Elite • 177

German Special Forces of World War II

GORDON WILLIAMSON   ILLUSTRATED BY MIKE CHAPPELL

Consultant editor Martin Windrow

First published in Great Britain in 2009 by Osprey Publishing,
Midland House, West Way, Botley, Oxford OX2 0PH, UK
443 Park Avenue South, New York, NY 10016, USA
Email: info@ospreypublishing.com

Print ISBN: 978 184603 920 1
ebook ISBN: 978 1 84908 136 8

Editor: Martin Windrow
Design: Ken Vail Graphic Design, Cambridge, UK (kvgd.com)
Typeset in Sabon and Myriad Pro
Index by Auriol Griffith-Jones
Originated by PDQ Digial Media Solutions Ltd, UK
Printed in China through World Print Ltd.

09 10 9 8 7 6 5 4 3 2 1

A CIP catalogue record for this book is available from the British Library

FOR A CATALOGUE OF ALL BOOKS PUBLISHED BY OSPREY MILITARY
AND AVIATION PLEASE CONTACT:

Osprey Direct, c/o Random House Distribution Center,
400 Hahn Road, Westminster, MD 21157
Email: uscustomerservice@ospreypublishing.com

Osprey Direct, The Book Service Ltd, Distribution Centre,
Colchester Road, Frating Green, Colchester, Essex, CO7 7DW
E-mail: customerservice@ospreypublishing.com

www.ospreypublishing.com

ARTIST'S NOTE

Readers may care to note that the original paintings from which the colour
plates in this book were prepared are available for private sale. All
reproduction copyright whatsoever is retained by the Publishers. All
enquiries should be addressed to:

Mike Chappell
13 route d'Alaigne
11300 Malras
France

The Publishers regret that they can enter into no correspondence upon
this matter.

PHOTO CREDITS

THE WOODLAND TRUST

Osprey Publishing are supporting the Woodland Trust, the UK's leading
woodland conservation charity, by funding the dedication of trees.

CONTENTS

GERMAN SPECIAL FORCES OF WORLD WAR II

INTRODUCTION

As with so many aspects of German government activities during the Third Reich, the formation of special-forces type units was seriously affected by the internecine struggles between not only the various branches of the armed forces, but also between the military and political intelligence services. The Army was the first to create such units when, under the auspices of Military Intelligence – the Abwehr – permission was given for the formation in October 1939 of the innocuously titled Lehr und Bau Kompanie zbV 800 ('Training and Construction Company on Special Duties 800'), soon to evolve into the renowned 'Brandenburgers'.

Even at this early stage there was considerable rivalry between the Abwehr, under Admiral Wilhelm Canaris, and the Reichsicherheitshauptamt (RSHA – Reich Main Security Office), at first under SS-Obergruppenführer Reinhard Heydrich and later SS-Ogruf Ernst Kaltenbrunner. The RSHA was the apparatus through which Reichsführer-SS Heinrich Himmler wielded the Nazi state's entire security and police organization; it considered itself the sole legitimate controller of intelligence, counter-intelligence and espionage activities, and – with some justification – it judged the Abwehr to be politically unreliable.

Born in Aplerbeck in 1887, Wilhelm Canaris had joined the Kaiserliche Marine in 1905 as an officer cadet, and during the early part of the Great War he served on the cruiser SMS *Dresden*. *Dresden* survived the battle of the Falkland Islands, but was eventually cornered by the Royal Navy in Chilean waters and was scuttled in March 1915; the crew were interned, but Canaris escaped and succeeded in returning to Germany. He subsequently joined the submarine service and became a successful U-boat commander. Canaris remained in the Navy after the war, becoming involved once again in intelligence work; in 1933 he was appointed as head of the Abwehr, being promoted to the rank of Konteradmiral in 1935.

From well before the outbreak of war Canaris, who despised Hitler and the Nazis, used his position to do everything within his power to interfere with the Führer's military ambitions. Indeed, he had been actively involved in the planning of two failed attempts on Hitler's life in 1938 and 1939. He is known to have worked to persuade Spain not to become involved in the war on Germany's side, and to deny German forces passage through Spanish territory for the proposed assault on Gibraltar. He was careful to appoint fellow

Admiral Wilhelm Canaris, shown here in his Kriegsmarine dress frock-coat. An enigmatic character, Canaris despised the Nazis, yet socialized with the head of the SD, SS-Obergruppenführer Reinhard Heydrich. General Heydrich was a former naval officer who had served under Canaris in the 1920s; he and Canaris' wife Erika shared a passionate interest in music, and the two families often dined together, while the two intelligence chiefs schemed against each other in private. (Bundesarchiv)

anti-Nazis into senior positions in the Abwehr, and by the mid point of the war he was making contact with senior Allied intelligence figures, including British intelligence chief Gen Stuart Menzies and the head of the American OSS, Gen William Donovan. His position as head of military intelligence enabled him to use his influence to help cover the tracks of the conspirators against Hitler.

Although the SS distrusted Canaris they were unable to produce proof of his activities, and had to settle for taking every opportunity to undermine him and the Abwehr in Hitler's eyes. During the early war years, when Germany's fortunes were riding high, Hitler was content to ignore the machinations of the SS against Canaris; but as the tides of war turned against Germany in 1943, and defeat followed defeat, the Führer was more willing to listen to the RSHA's complaints. Events began to come to a head in late 1943, when the Gestapo smashed an anti-Nazi group with close links to two members of the Abwehr based in Turkey; when the two Abwehr agents were summoned for interview they absconded and defected to the British. The RSHA lost no time in reporting this to Hitler, and when Canaris was summoned to explain these events to the Führer in person he passed a comment that the war was already lost anyway.

This was the last straw; in February 1944 Hitler transferred Canaris to a toothless post as head of the Office for Commercial and Economic Warfare, and placed the Abwehr (and with it, the Army special forces troops) under RSHA control as part of the Military Office in its Section VI.

The downfall of Canaris finally came with the abortive attempt on Hitler's life on 20 July 1944. Many Abwehr officers were executed for complicity in the plot; Canaris was at first placed under house arrest, and then held at Flossenburg concentration camp where, on 9 April 1945, he was hanged on Hitler's orders.

* * *

Well before its take-over of the Abwehr the SS had been working on the creation of a new unit that would be part of the Ausland-SD, the foreign espionage department of the Sicherheitsdienst or SS Security Service that was involved in military sabotage activities outside of Germany. The officer chosen to lead this new unit was a tough Austrian combat veteran; standing well over 6ft tall, powerfully built and with a face heavily scarred from duelling during his student days, Otto Skorzeny was an imposing figure by any standards.

His would be the one name that would eventually be directly linked with the special combat units of not just the Waffen-SS but all branches of the armed forces. After the effective dissolution of the Abwehr most of the Army Brandenburgers with special-forces training volunteered to transfer to Skorzeny's commando organization, the SS-Jagdverbände. He would also ultimately gain responsibility for combat operations by the K-Verbände of the Navy and the Luftwaffe's KG 200. His career offers one of the few examples of the inveterate plotting and empire-building of the SS having a beneficial effect on Germany's war effort, since there can be no doubt that Skorzeny was a highly effective leader who was greatly respected and admired by the men under his command.

Siegfried Grabert, shown here as an Oberleutnant, served as a Brandenburger from the first days of the war; he led Gruppe Ebbinghaus on the Polish frontier in September 1939, and was decorated with the Knight's Cross in June 1941 for capturing the bridge over the Vardar river at Axiopolis in Greece. He was also the first Brandenburger to win the Oakleaves to the Knight's Cross, posthumously in November 1942 after his death in action on the Eastern Front in July of that year. (Bundesarchiv)

THE ARMY

THE BRANDENBURGERS

Although an Army organization, the Brandenburgers were not under the direct control of the Oberkommando des Heeres, but were controlled by Admiral Canaris' Amt Ausland/Abwehr, a subordinate department of the Oberkommando der Wehrmacht (Joint Forces High Command).

Germany's premier special forces units had their origins in a small, temporary detachment created by Hauptmann Theodore von Hippel. Hippel had been a keen student of the guerrilla warfare tactics employed during World War I by officers such as T.E. Lawrence in Arabia and Paul von Lettow-Vorbeck in German East Africa, and

WILHELM CANARIS

The head of German military intelligence, Wilhelm Canaris, joined the Kaiserliche Marine in 1905 at the age of 17 and first experienced combat as a young naval officer during World War I, when he served first on the light cruiser *Dresden* and subsequently as the commander of a number of U-boats operating in the Mediterranean, where he succeeded in sinking four enemy ships totalling around 24,000 tons. His first experiences of intelligence work came when he was seconded to naval intelligence in Spain, where he was employed in gathering information on Allied shipping movements and in securing supplies for German shipping and submarines.

Canaris remained in the Navy at the end of World War I, and was involved with the post-war Freikorps. He reached the rank of Kapitän zur See in 1931, and served as executive officer on board the cruiser *Berlin*, an elderly warship that had survived the war and was recommissioned as a training ship. Later, he was appointed to command the old battleship *Schlesien*, also a training ship for naval cadets. At around this time he recommenced his involvement with naval intelligence.

In January 1935, Canaris was appointed head of military intelligence, being promoted to Konteradmiral at the end of that year. His powerful position gave him considerable insight into Hitler's military ambitions and he made strenuous efforts to prevent Hitler from attacking Czechoslovakia. Canaris in fact, exerted himself to interfere with Hitler's military ambitions on almost every level, and was directly involved in failed attempts to assassinate Hitler in 1938 and again in 1939. On the outbreak of war, the fears Canaris held over Hitler's intentions were brutally realized when he witnessed the murder of civilians during the attack on Poland. His subsequent protests were ignored and Canaris was warned not to interfere.

However, he arranged for detailed reports of Nazi atrocities to be forwarded to the Vatican, via a known Catholic figure in the German resistance, in the vain hope that the Papacy might use its influence to intervene. Canaris also passed information on via neutral nations such as Sweden, ensuring that the Allies were aware not only of Nazi atrocities, but of the resistance to Hitler inside Germany. Indeed, he is known to have clandestinely used the Abwehr's resources to enable various elements within German resistance circles to keep in contact with each other. Throughout his military career under the Nazis, Admiral Canaris did everything possible to frustrate Hitler's military operations, revealing important plans to the Allies and misleading Hitler as to the perceived intentions of the Allies.

Using his position of authority, Canaris ensured that those appointed to senior positions in the Abwehr staff were anti-Nazi, and he became directly involved in saving Jews who had fallen into the clutches of the Gestapo by personally intervening with Himmler and claiming that they were essential agents who had been working under cover for the Abwehr. It has been estimated that several hundred Jews were saved by the intervention of the Abwehr.

During 1943, Canaris had made direct contact with both the Americans and British in an attempt to convince them that there was serious resistance to Hitler within Germany, with suggestions including a surrender of the Wehrmacht to US forces, a ceasefire in the West, and either eliminating Hitler or handing him over to the Allies. Canaris' offers were rejected. He was once again directly involved in a further abortive attempt on Hitler's life in 1943, but it was only after the failed bomb plot in July 1944 that Hitler was finally convinced that Canaris was involved in the conspiracy against him.

Canaris was arrested and first held in chains by the Gestapo before being transferred to Flossenberg Concentration Camp in February 1945. Here he was kept on starvation rations, regularly beaten, mocked, tortured and humiliated. At no time did he reveal any information that could be used against his fellow conspirators. On 9 April 1945, following a bogus trial staged by two SS officers sent from Berlin, Canaris and several of his colleagues were stripped naked and led to the gallows. With their SS guards mocking them and hurling abuse, they were hanged and their bodies left to rot. Just two weeks later, the camp was liberated by US troops.

Oberleutnant Wilhelm Walther, wearing the Knight's Cross awarded on 24 June 1940 for his daring capture of the bridge over the Meuse at Gennep on the night of 9/10 May. (Josef Charita)

he came to be a trusted Abwehr subordinate and a close friend of Admiral Canaris. Von Hippel had no difficulty persuading his chief of the value of small, dedicated and highly trained special purpose units, and was given permission to create a small unit of saboteurs for employment during the German attack on Poland. Just two companies in strength, the unit was comprised largely of ethnic Germans from Central Europe (particularly western Poland and the Sudetenland). Known as Gruppe Ebbinghaus, this force, armed but dressed in civilian clothing, would precede German army units, preventing Polish attempts to demolish strategic targets and capturing important bridges.

The unit performed well and exceeded expectations but, surprisingly, was disbanded after the Polish surrender. Perhaps this decision was influenced by another operation involving irregular troops under the command of Abwehr officer Leutnant Hans-Albrecht Herzner, who had crossed from occupied Czechoslovakia into Poland on the original proposed launch date of the invasion, 26 August 1939. Hitler's decision to postpone the attack could not be communicated to the group, who launched an attack to seize the Jablunkov Pass and its strategically important railway tunnel. Only when the Germans seized the railway station at Mosty did they learn from the Poles that no state of war existed. Although Herzner and his men eventually returned safely, the Poles were certainly alerted to Germany's imminent intentions, and when war did break out a week later they were able to blow the railway tunnel before the Germans could attempt to seize it again.

THE WEST AND THE BALKANS, 1940–41

Canaris was nevertheless impressed by the success of these small irregular groups, and gave permission for the formation of a permanent unit on 15 October 1939. This Lehr und Bau Kompanie zbV 800 was located at Brandenburg, and would soon be known by the name of its home base.

From the beginning, recruitment for this unit was to be aimed at providing troops who could pass themselves off as non-Germans when carrying out covert operations. Finding those who could pass themselves off as Western Europeans such as Dutchmen, Belgians, Frenchmen and Scandinavians was no real problem, but Germany's ultimate territorial ambitions lay mainly towards the East. For this reason the stereotypical Aryan ideal was far from desirable, and recruits were specifically sought who had a Slavic appearance. Any who could speak Russian, Polish, Czech or Baltic languages and had detailed knowledge of the various regions of central and northern Europe were particularly valued; the lives of these future Brandenburgers would often

depend on being able to pass themselves off convincingly as citizens or soldiers of such states. Training was extremely tough; demolition and sabotage skills were taught along with survival techniques and fieldcraft, and intensive physical fitness training ensured that these troops had the highest levels of both physical and mental stamina.

Within just three months of its creation the new unit was enlarged from company to battalion strength. Its principal components were four companies formed along the lines of language abilities/ ethnic origins: 1 Kompanie, Baltic States/Russian; 2 Kompanie, English language/North and South Africa; 3 Kompanie, Sudeten German/Balkan; 4 Kompanie, Volksdeutsche (eastern ethnic German). A motorcycle reconnaissance platoon and a parachute-trained platoon were also available in support. A 'platoon' of Brandenburgers named the Nordzug, although actually at company strength, was committed for the invasion of Norway, but the first major operations came during the campaign in the West.

On 8 May 1940, a detachment of Brandenburgers from 4. Kompanie under the command of Lt Wilhelm Walther slipped over the border into Holland with some dressed in the uniforms of the Dutch Military Police. In the early hours of 10 May, Walther and those in Dutch uniform appeared near the bridge over the Meuse at Gennep, which had been prepared for demolition should the Germans attempt to cross. Apparently leading a number of unarmed German 'prisoners', they were able to approach the guard posts at the bridge and take the defenders by surprise. Three Brandenburgers were wounded, but the nearer guard posts were successfully overpowered. Walther, in Dutch uniform, then calmly approached the guard posts at the opposite end of the bridge; confused, and not sure exactly what

The bridge over the Meuse at Gennep, which was over 300 yards in length. Having seized the guardposts at one end of the bridge, Walther and his men – posing as Dutch Military Police escorting German prisoners – had to walk the full length of the bridge without cover; their subterfuge succeeded long enough for them to reach the opposite bank. (Bundesarchiv)

9

had happened on the far side of the river, the guards made the mistake of hesitating too long and allowing the Germans to come too close, and were swiftly overpowered. Walther succeeded in gaining complete control of the bridge just moments before the first German tanks rolled over.

At the same time, other Brandenburger groups had crossed into Luxemburg and captured the bridges over the Our river. In Belgium, detachments from 3. Kompanie carried out several audacious attacks which captured numerous road and rail bridges. Also in Holland, along with Walther's unit, a detachment commanded by Lt Kürschner captured the bridges over the Juliana Canal, while Lt Grabert stormed and seized the bridge at Nieuport in Belgium. Not every target was successfully captured, and some of the bridges were blown by their defenders before they could be seized; however, of 61 designated objectives, 42 were successfully achieved.

Following the victorious campaign in the West, the Brandenburgers were earmarked for use first in the planned invasion of Great Britain, and then for the proposed occupation of Gibraltar, both of which were ultimately cancelled. During the second half of 1940 the battalion was further expanded, with numerous new specialist sub-units including coastal raiders (Küstenjäger), and a company of expert skiers intended for use in operations in the far north. In December 1940 it was formally retitled as Lehr Regiment Brandenburg zbV 800. Like many special forces units, the Brandenburgers did not operate in fixed sub-units of conventional sizes, but rather in task-organized groups of however many men a particular operation required – a Brandenburg raiding group could range in strength from just a couple of men to a hundred or more.

The next major success for the regiment was in the lead-up to Operation *Marita*, when a team of Brandenburgers seized the major docks at Orsova on the Danube in the hours before the launching of the invasions of Greece and Yugoslavia in April 1941. A further detachment under Lt Grabert, disguised in Yugoslav uniforms, captured the bridge over the Vardar river after a brief but fierce battle with British troops.

NORTH AFRICA, 1942–43

The regiment's 13. or 'Tropical Company' was formed in October 1941 under Olt Friedrich von Koenen, a former colonial from German South-West Africa.

BRANDENBURGERS, 1939–42
1: Gruppe Ebbinghaus; Polish frontier, 1 September 1939
This clandestine force was recruited from among Polish-speaking Germans in Silesia. Commanded by Siegfried Grabert, they secured Katowice railway station and held it until the arrival of German regular troops. Civilian clothes were worn, and swastika armbands were only put on when on the point of going into action. Armament was limited to rifles and sub-machineguns, in this case a Polish-made Mauser rifle. The figure is taken from a group photo.
2: Gruppe Walther; Gennep, Holland, 10 May 1940
This soldier, from a photo taken on the Meuse bridge just after the action, wears the uniform of a Royal Netherlands Army sergeant of Military Police. This comprises the older two-pocket model of the tunic, with breeches, laced leggings and ankle boots; the rank chevron is worn on both forearms, and the

white lanyard identifies the Military Police. He has regulation infantry belt equipment and carries a Mannlicher carbine.
3: Abteilung von Fölkersam: Maikop, August 1942
This Brandenburger is dressed in the uniform of a sergeant of the NKVD, though with a Soviet M1940 steel helmet rather than the distinctive blue-and-red cap. The traditional *gymnastiorka* shirt-tunic has the pre-1943 piped fall collar, bearing rank patches: the sergeant's enamel bar on NKVD brick-red, piped raspberry-red. The NKVD's distinctive patch is worn on the left sleeve. Red-piped blue breeches and knee boots complete the uniform. Uniform regulations were often ignored in the NKVD – who sometimes chose not to display any rank insignia – and the fact that a sergeant is wearing an officer's 'Sam Browne'-style belt would not arouse suspicion. It supports a holstered Tokarev pistol and a magazine pouch for the PPSh41 sub-machine gun.

The company was 300 strong; half of it was based in Greece as 1.Kompanie of Sonderverband 288 (see below), and the other half at Naples. The first element crossed to North Africa with the Sonderverband in January 1942, the second in June; the two would serve for the next four months. Initially von Koenen's half-company was attached to Kampfgruppe Hecker along with the Italian 'San Marco' Marines, for an intended amphibious landing to cut the coast road behind British lines at Gazala. When this mission was cancelled Hecker's battle group was sent into action at Bir Hacheim on 29 May; however, the Brandenburg half-company was detached from Sonderverband 288, serving as a special reconnaissance force until El Alamein in October 1942.

Meanwhile, in late January 1942 the Abwehr had formed a separate unit, Sonderkommando Dora, under Obstlt Walter Eichler, for deep desert reconnaisance and raiding. In mid-June the second half-company of Brandenburgers, under Olt Conrad von Leipzig, arrived at Tripoli. Lavishly equipped with British vehicles and 40mm cannon captured at Tobruk, von Leipzig's unit worked with Sonderkommando Dora until the retreat following El Alamein. All the Brandenburgers then withdrew to Tunisia, where they joined up with a company-sized element from the Brandenburg I.

Born in Danzig in 1916, Hauptmann Freidrich ('Fritz') von Koenen led a 300-strong Brandenburger detachment known as 13. or 'Tropen-Kompanie' in North Africa. After the Axis capitulation in Tunisia in May 1943 the survivors of the then-Abteilung von Koenen managed to commandeer boats and cross to Sicily; their commander was awarded the Knight's Cross on 16 September 1943. They were later deployed to the Balkans, and Hptm von Koenen was killed when the car in which he was travelling was ambushed by Partisans in Herzogovina in August 1944. (Josef Charita)

Bataillon flown in on 5 December 1942; expanded to a strength of five companies, the combined unit was formally designated Abteilung von Koenen in January 1943.

On 26 December 1942 20 men were flown from Bizerta in three towed gliders to land behind Allied lines; they destroyed the bridge over the Wadi El Kebir at Sidi Bou Baker, and trekked more than 120 miles back to the safety of their own lines. On the same day, a ten-man team of Brandenburgers under Lt Hagenauer landed in a glider and successfully destroyed an Allied bridge north of Kasserine, but were then intercepted by a French armoured reconnaissance unit and captured. A further Allied-held bridge at Wadi El Melah was successfully destroyed by a Brandenburg detachment under the command of Lt Fuchs on 18 January 1943. Although this last target was a key link in the Allied supply route, by this point the German position in North Africa was so dismal that the successful mission made little impact on the situation. On 14 February, Abteilung von Koenen took part in the last German offensive in North Africa, the initially successful but costly operation at Sidi Bou Zid.

(One particularly audacious Brandenburg action in North Africa took place when the Küstenjäger of 5. Kompanie sent faked radio messages that duped the Allies into landing a party of troops from a submarine. They and their radio equipment were captured and the latter was used to carry out a second such deception, fooling the British into sending a second landing party, who were also promptly captured.)

SONDERVERBÄNDE 287 & 288

The entwined history of the Brandenburgers and Sonderverbände 287 and 288 demands further brief explanation. When Raschid Ali el Galiani led a revolt against the British occupiers of Iraq in April–May 1941 a German staff was formed to handle aid to Arab insurgents. These two units were raised at the Potsdam Ruinenberg barracks, with Brandenburgers forming a core for German personnel specially recruited from conventional units for their language skills and experience of life in relevant hot-weather regions. Before this process could be completed the Iraqi revolt was crushed, but the embryo units were judged potentially too useful to disband; there seems to have been an intention that once the Afrika Korps had defeated the British the Sonderverbände would move into Egypt and Persia, fomenting unrest and seizing the latter's oilfields for Germany.

In summer 1941 Sonderverband 287 was sent to Greece, where it received hot-weather training in the south; it also put out feelers to recruit pro-Axis Arabs from throughout the Middle East – largely Iraqis and Palestinians. It eventually reached a strength of three battalions, of which one would be sent to Tunisia, and the other two were committed to anti-partisan duty in the Caucasus and the Balkans.

The first 400 men of the all-German Sonderverband 288, commanded by Obst Otto Menton, were transferred from Greece to North Africa starting in January 1942; they included the 1. Kompanie of Brandenburgers (see above) to engage in sabotage and other special missions. By March the Sonderverband still had not received the other 1,400 men of its planned establishment, nor most of its vehicles or heavy weapons, and 1. Kompanie (von Koenen's Tropen-Kompanie of Brandenburgers) was detached and deployed for special missions, as described.

From May 1942 the rest of Sonderverband 288 – Kompanien 2. (Gebirgsjäger), 3. (Schützen), 4. (MG), 5. (Panzerjäger), 6. (Flak) and 7. (Pioniere), with a strong HQ, support and services company – were committed to action in a more or less conventional role, attached to 90. leichte Division. The unit was ordered to be re-organized into two battalions and redesignated PzGren Regiment (mot) Afrika in August 1942, and from February 1943 in Tunisia it was transferred to 164. leichte Afrika Division.

Two members of Sonderverband 288 with their Kubelwagen field car. The Feldwebel in the passenger seat wears regulation tropical dress; note the bleached field cap, a common affectation. The Sonderverband 287/288 right sleeve patch can also be seen. (Author's collection)

THE EASTERN FRONT

Back in Europe, by spring 1941 the Lehr-Regiment Brandenburg zbV 800 had expanded considerably, and now consisted of three battalions with numerous specialist companies. Regimental headquarters was in Berlin; I. Battailon (at Brandenburg) had 1. (training), 2., 3. and 4. Kompanien; the latter included a paratroop platoon, later expanded to a full paratroop company. II. Battalion (at Baden) had 5. (mountain), 6. (reconnaissance), 7. and 8. Kompanien (both mountain). III. Battalion (also at Baden) had 9. to 12. Kompanien. A signals company was formed in early 1941, but its troops were distributed to other sub-units within the regiment. A Küstenjäger company was formed in early 1942 from 4. Kompanie. A former 'V-Leute' (intelligence agents) company that had been created in the spring of 1940 was merged with 1. Kompanie and the Interpreter Company to form a new 'V-Leute' battalion in 1942.

The Brandenburgers were to see heavy action during the early stages of Operation *Barbarossa*. The regiment's constituent units were allocated separately: I. Btl to Army Group South, elements of II. Btl to Army Groups North and South, and III. Btl to Army Group Centre. Within the Army Groups the battalions were further sub-divided, individual companies being temporarily task-allocated to various divisions. As would be expected, the Brandenburgers went into action ahead of the main forces, often disguised in enemy uniforms and tasked with seizing vital objectives such as bridges; they achieved considerable success, but often at the cost of heavy casualties.

Elements of I. Btl succeeded in capturing vital bridges over the San, Bug, Styr and Dniepr rivers, and were involved in the capture of Lemberg alongside mountain troops of 1. Gebirgs Division. Troops from II. Btl captured bridges over the Dniepr and Dvina rivers, and III. Btl seized no fewer than eight bridges in a single day. Often, after having achieved their initial special objectives, the Brandenburgers then fought on as conventional troops alongside the units to which they were attached.

One of the most audacious Brandenburg raids on the Eastern Front came in August 1942. Led by Freiherr Adrian von Fölkersam, a detachment of Brandenburgers some 60 strong approached the Soviet-controlled oilfields at Maikop in captured Red Army trucks and dressed in the uniform of the feared NKVD security troops. They infiltrated Soviet lines, and when they ran into a large number of Red Army deserters they 'stayed in role', rounding them up and used their arrest as a perfect screen for passing through Soviet territory. The captured men indeed believed that they had been arrested by the NKVD, and when von Fölkersam encountered other Soviet troops he successfully passed himself off to the general in charge of Maikop's defences as an NKVD major returning with a number of 'traitors'. Incredibly, von Fölkersam was then given a guided tour of Maikop's defences.

B **BRANDENBURGERS, 1943–45**

1: Küstenjäger; Aegean islands, summer 1943

The coastal raiders of the Küstenjäger Abteilung of the Brandenburg regiment were trained by the Kriegsmarine, and indeed included several former Navy personnel. The sun-bleached field cap, shirt and shorts worn by this helmsman of an assault boat (Sturmboot) operating in the Aegean are probably naval khaki issue; he also wears canvas and leather tropical ankle boots, and his kapok-filled life jacket hides a webbing belt with a holstered Walther P38 pistol.

2: Feldwebel, 15. (Fallschirm) Kompanie; Leros, November 1943

This veteran NCO, from a photo taken on Leros, wears standard Army-issue tropical uniform items – the original olive shades differentially faded – but with European-issue black leather equipment and ankle boots. His shoulder straps of rank are piped in Jäger-green; he wears the original Army version of the Paratrooper Badge, and his awards are the ribbon of the Iron Cross 2nd Class, the pin-back 1st Class, and the Infantry Assault Badge. His weapon is the MP40 sub-machine gun.

3: Unteroffizier, Fallschirmjäger Kompanie/ Bataillon; Eastern Front, 1944

Although the expansion to divisional status and the commitment in conventional roles robbed the Brandenburgers of much of their special-forces character, in February 1944 a parachute battalion was formed within the division. Some of these jump-trained troops took part in the abortive attack on Tito's headquarters at Drvar alongside SS-FJ Bn 500. Taken from a photo, this figure wears the M1943 universal field cap, and the field-grey version of the 'special uniform for armoured troops', which by this date was being issued quite widely to Panzergrenadier units. The 'wrap-over' jacket is factory-fitted with the subdued universal pattern of breast eagle and collar *Litzen*, and the shoulder straps are now grey rayon. rather than dark green badge-cloth. He wears the Wound Badge in Black, and an embroidered version of the Army Paratrooper Badge.

1

2

3

Two Brandenburgers photographed with comrades from the Kriegsmarine and Luftwaffe after the capture of the Greek island of Leros in November 1943. The soldier in the centre is a decorated combat veteran with the Iron Cross 1st Class; note that he also wears the Army version of the Paratrooper Badge, so is presumably a member of the regiment's 15. (Fallschirm) Kompanie. (Mike Bischoff)

On 8 August, with the main German forces just a few miles away, the Brandenburgers launched a grenade attack on the Maikop communications centre, correctly assuming that the Soviets would believe that they were under artillery attack. In a monstrous bluff, von Fölkersam then persuaded the Russian defenders that they were to withdraw, since a major enemy attack was about to overwhelm them. With no communications to allow them to confirm this, the Russians accepted the orders of this senior officer in the dreaded NKVD and withdrew, allowing the Germans to enter the city without a shot being fired on 9 August 1942.

At the same time another Brandenburg unit, also dressed in Soviet uniforms and commanded by Lt Ernst Prohaska, played the part of a rapidly retreating Red Army unit, speeding in captured Soviet trucks towards the strategically important bridge at Bjelaja. Seeing what they thought were their own troops in full retreat in the face of a powerful German force, the bridge defenders abandoned their positions and fled, allowing Prohaska's men to disarm the demolition charges which had been set in preparation for blowing the bridge. Both von Fölkersam and Prohaska were decorated with the Knight's Cross of the Iron Cross for their actions that day.

Brandenburg units were employed for many such special operations in the months to come, and from late 1942 were also frequently used on anti-partisan operations. However, in Germany the struggle between their controlling department, the Abwehr, and the SS was approaching its climax. Although there was considerable dissatisfaction that what had begun as a special operations formation was by now being used, piecemeal, in a conventional role, the decision was taken to remove the Brandenburg regiment from the control of the Abwehr and enlarge it. As a first stage in this process, from early 1943 onwards Brandenburg units were collectively redesignated as Sonderverbände Brandenburg; the headquarters element became Sonderverband 800, the former battalions Sonderverbände 801, 802 and 803, and a new Sonderverband 804 was also created. These units fought on in the East until late March/early April 1943, by which point virtually all had been withdrawn to Germany to be reformed.

DIVISIONAL STATUS

The new division officially formed from these units did not fight as a single entity, its units being detached for operational use as and when required. The expansion naturally meant that the high standards of selection used when recruiting for a special operations unit could no longer be sustained, and the quality of recruits fell. However, the surviving veteran personnel were still highly skilled and trained in special operations work, and Brandenburg retained many of its specialist sub-units as cadres for new units such as the Küstenjäger and parachute battalions.

During the first six months of its existence as a nominal division the Brandenburg continued to provide personnel for special operations. On 3 October 1943 members of the Küstenjäger Bataillon landed on the Greek island of Kos, which had been occupied by British troops, and recaptured the island. On 12 November the Küstenjäger were in action once again, together with 15. (Fallschirm) Kompanie, acting together with Luftwaffe and other Army units in an attack on the British-held island of Leros. The fighting was by no means as easy as it had been on Kos; the British held on tenaciously, and the Brandenburgers were forced to beat off several counter-attacks before the arrival of German reinforcements swung the balance; the British were finally forced to surrender on 17 November.

By late 1943, the Brandenburg Division had the following order of battle: divisional headquarters; Jäger (light infantry) regiments 1 & 2; artillery regiment; Panzer regiment; engineer battalion; anti-tank battalion; Flak battalion; signals battalion, and reconnaissance battalion. There was a parachute company, later raised (nominally) to a battalion, and although by now a much smaller proportion of the unit personnel were volunteers trained for special missions, Brandenburgers were still taking part in such operations – for example, some volunteers participated alongside SS-Fallschirmjäger Bataillon 500 in Operation 'Rösselsprung', the attack on Tito's headquarters at Drvar.

On 13 September 1944, the division was formally renamed as Panzergrenadier Division 'Brandenburg'. Re-forming in the new role took some months, and in the course of this period the Küstenjäger and Fallschirmjäger elements were withdrawn. By this time many of the original surviving Brandenburgers were decidedly unhappy with the changes to their

Baron Adrian von Fölkersam, the Brandenburger officer who in summer 1942 bluffed his men's way through Soviet lines defending the Maikop oilfields while dressed as an officer of the dreaded NKVD security troops. He was one of the Brandenburgers who subsequently requested transfer to Skorzeny's SS-Jagdverbände, and continued to serve with special forces throughout the war. Fölkersam led Kampfgruppe X of PzBde 150 in the Ardennes, where he was wounded at Malmédy on 21 December 1944, and suffered a fatal head wound on the Eastern Front exactly a month later. (Josef Charita)

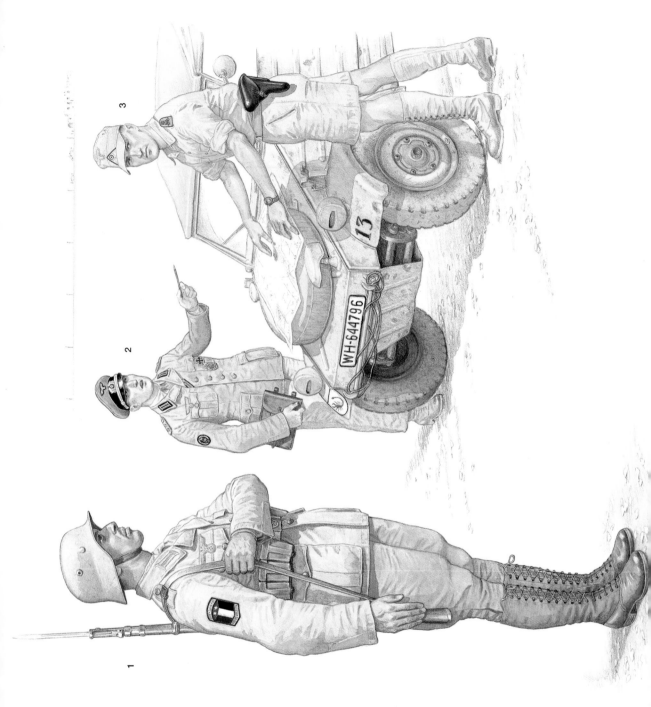

unit and objected to being used as conventional grenadiers, and as a result many hundreds of them requested transfer to the SS-controlled commando units under Maj Otto Skorzeny. Panzergrenadier Division 'Brandenburg' thereafter fought exclusively on the Eastern Front, where it eventually became part of Panzerkorps 'Grossdeutschland'; after many bitterly contested battles, in the final days of the war its remnants were forced to retreat into Czechoslovakia, where it surrendered. The luckiest of its survivors managed to make their way west, but many of their less fortunate comrades ended up in Soviet captivity.

SPECIAL INSIGNIA

A special cufftitle was authorized for the Brandenburg units on 17 August 1944. This was 3.2cm wide and cut from dark bottle-green cloth, with edging in silver-grey 'Russia braid', and bore in the centre the title *Brandenburg* machine-embroidered in silver-grey thread Fraktur script.The band was to be worn on the right cuff, but photographs of it in wear are quite rare. In any case, by the time of its introduction most of those who might have received it were serving in the role of conventional infantry rather than special forces.

Jäger Regimente 1 and 2 in the PzGren Div 'Brandenburg' wore on the upper right sleeve the Jäger patch. This was an oval of dark green woollen cloth, bearing in the centre a sprig of three light green oakleaves on brown stems, all surrounded by a twisted 'rope' border in very pale green.

Brandenburgers serving with both Sonderverband 287 and 288 wore on the upper right sleeve an oval dark green patch woven with a white swastika at the base; from this two palm-branches rose to enclose a white palm tree at the left and a pale yellow rising sun at the right.

The special patch worn on the upper right sleeve by members of Sonderverbände 287 and 288. The backing is in dark green, with off-white woven details and a pale yellow rising sun. Original examples of this insignia are naturally extremely rare, and it is much counterfeited. (Author's collection)

THE WAFFEN-SS

THE SKORZENY COMMANDOS

Although the Waffen-SS when on active service in the field came under the control of the Oberkommando der Wehrmacht, and Skorzeny and many of his troops were Waffen-SS personnel, the direct chain of command for his units was from Amt IV (SD-Ausland) of the RSHA, headed by SS-Obergruppenführer Ernst Kaltenbrunner, who was directly responsible to RFSS Heinrich Himmler.

In 1942 the RSHA created its own special unit, closely modelled on the Brandenburgers but manned only by trusted and politically reliable members of the SS. The Austrian-born SS-Hauptsturmführer Otto Skorzeny was appointed to command this new SS-Sonderverband zbV Friedenthal in April 1943. Captain Skorzeny had been recommended by his fellow Austrian SS-Ogruf Kaltenbrunner, who knew Skorzeny personally from pre-war times in Vienna. (Despite their own fervent support of the Nazi cause, Kaltenbrunner and Skorzeny had actually saved the life of the Austrian President Wilhelm Miklas on 12 March 1938, when they prevented his murder by a group of Nazi thugs.)

Otto Skorzeny was born in Vienna on 12 June 1908. On graduating from university with a degree in engineering, he formed his own company. He had

Oberleutnant Max Wandrey, one of the Brandenburgers, who landed with the Küstenjäger to take part in the capture of Leros. Wandrey was personally responsible for capturing the British Brig Robert Tilney; he is seen here wearing the German Cross in Gold and the Knight's Cross, to which he was also awarded the Oakleaves in 1945. (Josef Charita)

joined the Austrian Nazi Party whilst still a student, and by the time Austria was annexed by Germany in 1938 he was an active member of the SS. On the outbreak of war Skorzeny volunteered for the Luftwaffe, but at 1.92m (6ft 3½in) he was considered too tall, and at 31 too old, for pilot training. He was posted to the communications branch, but transferred to the SS-Verfügungstruppe at the earliest opportunity, and served in the 'Leibstandarte SS Adolf Hitler' Regiment during the campaign in the West. By the opening of the campaign against the Soviet Union in June 1941 Skorzeny was serving in the 'Das Reich' Division. He saw considerable combat, earning the Iron Cross First Class; late in 1941 he took a fragment wound in the head but refused to be evacuated, insisting on staying with his unit until his condition deteriorated to the extent that he had to be shipped back to a hospital in Vienna.

On recovery, he was posted to a staff job in Berlin whilst recuperating. Here he used his time to study commando tactics, and became a keen exponent of the concept of small, highly trained teams operating behind enemy lines. Now, in his new role, he would have plentiful opportunities to put his ideas into practice.

In June 1943, Skorzeny found himself in command of a newly formed unit designated SS-Jägerbataillon 502, and was given permission to recruit top quality men not just from within the SS but also from the other armed services. The unit would comprise three companies of German troops and one of foreign volunteers. (In time, as his influence grew, Skorzeny would also have SS-Fallschirmjäger Bataillon 500 / 600 placed under his command, and would even become involved in developing special weapons units with the Kriegsmarine's K-Verbände and the Luftwaffe's Kampfgeschwader 200.) Soon after being appointed to command the new unit Skorzeny was handed his first mission, which would start him on his climb from relative obscurity to become one of Germany's most famous soldiers.

On 24 July 1943 the Italian dictator Benito Mussolini had been forcibly deposed by his own Fascist Grand Council and placed under arrest. Whatever Mussolini's failings as an ally Hitler refused to see his fellow dictator humbled and imprisoned, and after considering a number of candidates to lead a rescue mission he personally selected Skorzeny for the task. On 3 September the British landings in Italy began, and on the 8th Marshal Badoglio announced the Armistice that had been signed with the Allies five days earlier.

Skorzeny flew to Italy to take command of a mixed group of around 20 Luftwaffe and 50 Waffen-SS troops. Intelligence sources had learned that Mussolini was being held at the Campo Imperatore resort hotel on the Gran Sasso mountain to the north-east of Rome. The only direct route up the mountain was by a funicular railway, which would hardly be suitable for a surprise assault; but aerial reconnaissance revealed that close to the hotel on the plateau there was a level area that looked as if it might possibly be suitable for a glider landing. Skorzeny's force, now just over 100 strong, was split into three groups for the mission: Skorzeny would lead a gilder-borne landing on the Gran Sasso, while a second group under the Luftwaffe's Maj Mors would seize the funicular railway in the valley to prevent any reinforcements reaching the Italian guard force, and a third group would rescue Mussolini's family from a separate location. In order to conceal their identity the Waffen-SS troops involved in the operation all wore Luftwaffe uniforms.

At just after 2pm on 12 September 1943, Skorzeny landed on the Gran Sasso in the first of the gliders; the landing zone was much rougher than anticipated, but the aircraft crash-landed successfully just 15 yards from the building. A startled Carabinieri guard nearby surrendered immediately, and as the other gliders made their approach Skorzeny stormed into the building, surprising another guard and quickly smashing his radio set. Returning outside and moving around the building, Skorzeny spotted Mussolini at a window and signalled him to stay back. Re-entering the hotel, Skorzeny and

SS-Obergruppenführer Ernst Kaltenbrunner, the former Higher SS Police Leader in Vienna who was appointed in Janurary 1943 to head the Reich Main Security Office. (For eight months after the assassination of his predecessor SS-Ogruf Heydrich no successor had been named; Himmler tried to run the RSHA personally, for fear of appointing another over-ambitious deputy.) A fellow Viennese and personal acquaintance of Otto Skorzeny, Kaltenbrunner recommended him to Hitler as an ideal commander for the special mission to rescue Mussolini. (Josef Charita)

DFS230 glider from Skorzeny's team after landing safely on the Gran Sasso on 12 September 1943; Skorzeny himself rode in the first glider down. The DFS230 was capable of carrying ten fully equipped soldiers. (Bundesarchiv)

his men quickly disarmed a group of guards, ran upstairs, found Mussolini's room and captured the two officers who were guarding him. The whole operation had taken less than five minutes so far.

The German troops in the following gliders had less luck with their landings, one aircraft being smashed to pieces on the rocks. The Germans then became embroiled in a short firefight with other Carabinieri defending the hotel, but one of the officers who had been guarding Mussolini was persuaded to order the remaining Italians to surrender to avoid further bloodshed. The German detachment tasked with seizing the station for the funicular railway at the base of the mountain had also succeeded, and soon joined Skorzeny on the plateau.

Having achieved his initial goal of securing Mussolini's release, and with the plateau secured, Skorzeny was now faced with the task of moving the dictator to safety in German-held territory. Rather than risk being intercepted while moving overland, it had been planned to fly him out from the nearby Aquila de Abruzzi airfield, or from the foot of the mountain near the funicular railway; in the event, it was decided to take off from the mountain itself. A skilled Luftwaffe pilot, Lt Gerlach, succeeded in landing a light Fieseler Storch spotter aircraft on the plateau, but was disconcerted when the giant Skorzeny insisted on joining him and the corpulent Mussolini for the flight off the mountain. With the pilot, Mussolini and Skorzeny crammed inside the tiny, low-powered

Skorzeny is seen here dressed in a Luftwaffe tropical uniform immediately after freeing Mussolini from his captors on the Gran Sasso. The daring landing by glider and the rescue of Hitler's closest ally would be fully exploited by Goebbel's Propaganda Ministry, and made Skorzeny a household name in Germany. Note that some Italian personnel seem quite happy to be included in the photo. (US National Archives)

aircraft barely made it off the plateau, but thanks to Gerlach's skill it landed safely at Practica di Mare airfield, where Skorzeny and Mussolini boarded a Heinkel He111 which flew them to an airfield near Vienna.

By any standards the rescue of Mussolini was an audacious operation, brilliantly executed; Skorzeny was promoted SS-Sturmbannführer (major), and he and Gerlach were both awarded the Knight's Cross. However, although it had been very much a combined operation, under the overall operational command of the Luftwaffe and employing more Luftwaffe than Waffen-SS personnel, it was to be the Waffen-SS element who were hailed as heroes, while the Luftwaffe's contribution was largely ignored.

(The previous winter it had been considered whether Skorzeny and his men should be used in a similar operation to kidnap Marshal Petain from Vichy-controlled southern France and move him to the German-occupied area, but in the event this operation had been cancelled.)

BERLIN, JULY 1944

Skorzeny and his men were briefly involved in the suppression of the abortive uprising following the bomb attempt on Hitler's life on 20 July 1944. Skorzeny was about to depart Berlin for Vienna when news of the attempt reached him and he was ordered to remain in the capital. His actions that night initially consisted mainly of visiting various commands and advising them not to get involved in what was a highly confused situation, and to remain on the alert in their barracks. After sending a company of his men from their base at Friedenthal to protect the SD headquarters he led others to the headquarters of the Reserve Army, where he met with Maj Ernst-Otto Remer of the 'Grossdeutschland' Division. Together Skorzeny's and Remer's men occupied the plotters' Bendlerstrasse headquarters to prevent anyone leaving. By this time four of them, including Claus von Stauffenberg, had already been executed (mainly to prevent them being interrogated under torture and forced to reveal the identities of others involved in the conspiracy). Skorzeny put a halt to the executions and arrested the remaining suspects before transferring them to Gestapo custody. Skorzeny then acted as temporary commander at Reserve Army headquarters until the situation was brought under control. This display of loyalty to the regime served to increase even further Skorzeny's standing in the eyes of Hitler.

The attempt on his life destroyed Hitler's already decreasing trust in the Army, and plans were put in place to dismantle the 'special forces' character of the Brandenburgers and convert the unit into a conventional combat force; from now on it would be SS-Stubaf Skorzeny who would lead Germany's 'commandos'. His Jägerbataillon was enlarged to become a Jagdverband of six battalions, into which nearly 2,000 men of former Brandenburg units and individual volunteers were transferred.

THE EASTERN FRONT: WALTER GIRG

One of Skorzeny's most able officers at this time was the young SS-Untersturmführer Walter Girg, who in late August 1944 was serving as a platoon commander in 1./ SS-Jäger Bataillon 502. Girg had been tasked with leading a reconnaissance mission deep into enemy territory, to disrupt supply lines and block passes through the Carpathians that would be useful to the advancing Red Army. Having achieved some success in disrupting the enemy advance and also saving some of the ethnic Germans living in the region, Girg disguised himself as a Romanian and took part in the 'celebration' of the Soviet advance. Subsequently, however, he and his men were discovered and taken prisoner near Brasov. After severe beatings the Germans were being lined up to be shot when an artillery barrage distracted the Soviets, and the

Germans made a run for it. Girg escaped despite being wounded in the foot while making his getaway, and the information that he and his men had gathered during the course of the operation was instrumental in allowing the Germans to avoid the encirclement of an entire corps. Girg received a well-deserved promotion to SS-Obersturmführer.

Thereafter SS-Ostuf Girg took command of an armoured unit operating behind enemy lines using captured Soviet tanks. On one occasion, while making his way back to the German lines through Soviet-held territory, Girg was intercepted near Kolberg by German troops who suspected him of being one of the so-called 'Seydlitz' troops (Communist-sympathising German turncoats recruited by the Soviets from among prisoners of war). His captors refused to believe him when he explained his true identity; he was given a summary trial for treason and sentenced to death, and a signal from Skorzeny confirming Girg's true identity arrived only just in time to prevent his execution.

Walter Girg was promoted to SS-Hauptsturmführer, and after Operation *Panzerfaust* in October 1944 he was awarded the Knight's Cross. Thereafter it was said that even when in disguise during covert operations Girg wore his decoration at all times, hidden under a scarf when necessary. He survived the war, after receiving the Oakleaves to his Knight's Cross.

BUDAPEST, OCTOBER 1944

Skorzeny's next major covert operation was codenamed Operation *Panzerfaust*. The SD had learned that Admiral Miklós Horthy, the Regent of German-allied Hungary, had sent LtGen Faragho to Moscow to seek a

Skorzeny (left) and his immediate controller SS-Ogruf Kaltenbrunner flank Hitler as they stroll through the wooded area surrounding Hitler's headquarters at Rastenburg, the so-called 'Wolfs Lair'. During this visit Skorzeny was presented with the Pilot-Observer Badge with Diamonds by Hermann Göring, in compliment to his co-operation with the Luftwaffe during the Gran Sasso mission. (US National Archives)

Waffen-SS troops under Otto Skorzeny's command on Castle Hill in Budapest, with one of the King Tiger tanks seconded from schwere Panzer Abteilung 503 for Operation *Panzerfaust*, the seizure of Admiral Horthy's palace and other government buildings. The casual attitude of the troops suggests that this photo was taken after the successful conclusion of the mission. (Bundesarchiv)

separate peace with the Soviet Union. Skorzeny's objective was to occupy the Hungarian seat of government, on Castle Hill in Budapest; it was hoped that a powerful German show of force would intimidate the Hungarians into remaining loyal to Germany under the leadership of Ferenc Szálasi of the extreme right-wing Arrow-Cross movement. Skorzeny's force would include SS-Jagdverband Mitte, a battalion of SS paratroops, another of Luftwaffe paratroops and a battalion of motorized infantry. Skorzeny was issued with written orders signed by Hitler personally, instructing all military and state agencies to provide whatever support or assistance he requested (this document made Maj Skorzeny temporarily one of the most powerful men in the Reich).

D **SKORZENY COMMANDOS, 1943–44**

1: SS-Hauptsturmführer Skorzeny; Italy, September 1943
Otto Skorzeny is seen here as he was photographed soon after the rescue of Mussolini from the Gran Sasso. Although some photos show him wearing a Luftwaffe tropical cap, another features this white-covered summer version of the Luftwaffe officer's service cap. The uniform is the Luftwaffe tropical shirt and trousers in golden-tan, with tropical ankle boots and a Luftwaffe brown belt. He wears Luftwaffe officer's flying branch shoulder straps of his equivalent rank of Hauptmann; the breast eagle is the factory-fitted all-ranks Luftwaffe tropical version in pale blue-grey on a tan triangular backing. At the throat Skorzeny displays his newly awarded Knight's Cross.

2: SS-Untersturmführer Schwerdt; Italy, 12 September 1943
Schwerdt, one of Skorzeny's officers on the Gran Sasso mission, was photographed standing beside Il Duce. He too wears Luftwaffe tropical uniform: in his case, a tropical field cap with silver officer's piping, and the four-pocket tunic with Luftwaffe officer's shoulder straps of his equivalent rank of Leutnant. The

photo shows an Iron Cross 1st Class, a General Assault Badge and a Wound Badge in Silver. Armed with a Fallschirmgewehr 42 automatic rifle, he is wearing a brown belt, black braces, and an intriguing pair of magazine pouches resembling those for the old MP28 sub-machine gun.

3: Einheit Stielgau; Ardennes, 17 December 1944
This commando, attempting to misdirect traffic and sow confusion behind American lines during Operation *Greif*, is disguised as a sergeant of US Army Military Police. He wears the M1 helmet with white 'MP' and band, a greatcoat with rank chevrons and an 'MP' brassard, and double-buckle boots. His weapon is a captured Thompson M1928A1 sub-machine gun, with a triple magazine pouch on a web pistol belt. Only a handful of the Germans in these three-man jeep teams could speak genuinely convincing American English; like most of his comrades, this one will probably end up in front of a firing squad.

Initially, Skorzeny and some of his staff officers travelled incognito to Budapest posing as civilians. There, it was decided to abduct Horthy's surviving son (also named Miklós, and party to his father's intentions) as a hostage to ensure the Regent's co-operation. On 15 October, while he was engaged in a meeting with Yugoslav agents, the younger Horthy was seized after a brief gun battle with his Hungarian guards, and was later flown to Germany.

SS-Hauptsturmführer Skorzeny at the Führerhauptquartier with Hitler, who personally decorated him with the Knight's Cross. Skorzeny's great height is particularly noticeable in this photo. (US National Archives)

The approaches to Castle Hill were mined and its garrison reinforced as the Hungarians prepared to defy Hitler; at 1pm Admiral Horthy issued a proclamation announcing that Hungary had concluded a separate peace treaty with the USSR and that the Hungarian Army at the front should cease fire.

Skorzeny was faced with a possibly difficult and costly assault on the well-defended fortress of Castle Hill. The German reaction to the Hungarian proclamation began with sealing off railway stations and other strategic locations to ensure that German military traffic heading for the front could pass unimpeded. A cordon of Waffen-SS troops was also placed around Castle Hill, drawn from the 22. Freiwilligen Kavallerie Division der SS 'Maria Theresia', which included a number of Hungarian volunteers; the Army's Panzer Brigades 109 and 110 also occupied the city, and Skorzeny determined that an assault on the palace precincts would begin at 6am the following day. He rebuffed an attempt to parley by Hungarian forces on Castle Hill, insisting that only a retraction of the national ceasefire was acceptable; at 5pm the order was duly countermanded by the Army chief-of-staff, ColGen János Vörös.

At 6am on 16 October, Skorzeny led forward a column of Waffen-SS troops supported by a number of giant King Tiger tanks from the Army's sPzAbt 503, and by engineers with some tracked, remote-control 'Goliath' demolition crawlers. The German column moved up the hill without challenge and reached the plateau outside the castle; three Hungarian tanks sited there wisely chose not to engage the King Tigers, which then smashed their way through a stone barricade into the castle courtyard.

Skorzeny and his men ran into the castle, and ordered a surprised Hungarian officer to escort them to the general-commandant, who acceded to Skorzeny's demands to surrender the castle and avoid major bloodshed. The

Waffen-SS troops armed with Panzerfausts in the courtyard of Buda Castle on 15 October 1944, after the surrender of the Hungarian guards – note the litter of discarded Hungarian weapons and equipment. In the background can be seena Hungarian 'Nimrod' armoured vehicle armed with a 40mm gun; wisely, none of the Hungarian crews offered any resistance to sPzAbt 503's Tiger B tanks. (Bundesarchiv)

entire operation had taken only some 30 minutes and had involved only very limited casualties in minor skirmishing: the Hungarians lost three dead and 15 wounded, and the Germans four dead and 12 wounded. Admiral Horthy officially abdicated at 8.15am; he slipped out of the castle before it was stormed and surrendered himself to SS-Ogruf Karl von Pfeffer-Wildenbruch, the Austrian commander of IX SS Mountain Corps. Skorzeny was subsequently ordered to collect Horthy from Pfeffer-Wildenbruch, and personally escorted him back to Germany.

Skorzeny's Jagdverbände wore no special uniforms or insignia; this photo taken during Operation 'Panzerfaust' shows that their clothing and equipment were typical Waffen-SS standard issue. (Bundesarchiv)

E SKORZENY COMMANDOS, 1944–45

1: SS-Obersturmbannführer Skorzeny; Schwedt bridgehead, February 1945

A photo taken on the Oder front shows Skorzeny looking somewhat haggard, and without his distinctive moustache; in the last week of December 1944 he had suffered another head wound from a shell fragment. He wears the officer's version of the M1943 universal field cap with silver crown piping, and Waffen-SS insignia divided between the front and the left side. His Knight's Cross and rank insignia can just be seen in the neck of the Waffen-SS padded reversible camouflage parka in an 'autumn/winter' pattern, and the matching overtrousers are confined by canvas anklets above a pair of Gebirgstruppe mountain boots. Note that he retains the SS officer's belt with its distinctive circular clasp.

2: SS-Oberscharführer, SS-Jagdverband Mitte; Budapest, October 1944

Photos show that nothing distinguished the men of this unit from any other Waffen-SS infantry – indeed, apart from the M1942 'raw edge' steel helmet without insignia, this senior NCO has a distinctly early-war look. He wears an M1936-type tunic with green badge-cloth collar facing and shoulder straps, and old-style marching boots; the original photo shows the stick-grenades (and also the use by one NCO of the pre-1943 'Schiffchen' field cap). He is armed with the MP40, and carries a Panzerfaust 60.

3: SS-Hauptsturmführer Walter Girg, SS-Jagdverband Mitte; Budapest, October 1944

This swashbuckling captain, renowned for daring operations behind Soviet lines, would be decorated with the Knight's Cross after Operation Panzerfaust; he would later be captured by the Red Army but would escape, earning himself the Oakleaves before the end of the war. He wears absolutely standard Waffen-SS officer's service dress with the officer's greatcoat, the cap and shoulder straps piped in infantry white. Unusually for an officer he is heavily armed, with two sets of magazine pouches for his MP40.

Skorzeny (centre) with ...an von Fölkersam and Walter Girg on the esplanade outside Buda Castle following the successful conclusion of the Horthy operation. At left is a member of the Hungarian Arrow-Cross party, the extreme right-wing movement that remained loyal to Germany, and whose leader Ferenc Szálasi was installed as prime minister after the coup against Admiral Horthy. (Bundesarchiv)

The success of this latest mission brought Skorzeny promotion to lieutenant-colonel, and the award of the German Cross in Gold. After the award was made personally by Hitler at the Führerhauptquartier on 22 October, the Führer briefed him on plans for the forthcoming offensive in the Ardennes and discussed what was to be Skorzeny's part in this operation.

THE ARDENNES, DECEMBER 1944

Under the code name Operation *Greif*, Skorzenny was to create – in just five weeks – a force designated Panzerbrigade 150; the designation was based on the intent that the unit would be equipped with substantial numbers of captured Allied armoured vehicles. Skorzeny was to assemble a force dressed in captured US uniforms and riding in captured vehicles; their mission would be to infiltrate Allied lines once these had been disrupted by the initial armoured breakthrough, and advance in the guise of retreating US troops to seize two strategic bridges over the River Meuse. While the bulk of Skorzeny's brigade would be committed to pushing through to capture the designated targets, smaller commando teams of English-speakers, travelling in captured jeeps, would carry out in-depth reconnaissance, posing as US troops as they spread false information, disrupted communications and generally caused as much alarm and confusion as possible. (It is interesting to note that when orders went out requesting English-speaking volunteers, lax German security revealed that they were to work with Skorzeny, yet when the Allied intelligence services became aware of these appeals they failed to grasp their significance.)

Unsurprisingly, in the event nowhere near the required number of vehicles for the planned three battalions became available at the Grafenwöhr training base. The brigade would go into action with just one captured American M4 Sherman tank, backed by German PzKw V Panthers and StuG III assault guns modified with thin sheet metal panels to approximate the silhouette of

American AFVs, and finished in olive drab paintwork and large white stars. Only four captured American armoured cars and two half-tracks were available, and these too had to be supplemented by disguised German vehicles. Larger numbers of Allied 'softskin' vehicles were scraped together, but not nearly as many serviceable cars and trucks as requested. Suitable captured uniforms and weapons were also in woefully short supply, and only key personnel could be properly equipped.

Quite apart from materiel shortages, it proved impossible to build a unit with the required strength of 3,300 men from specially recruited volunteers in the time available. Skorzeny managed to enlist only about 400 English speakers, of whom only around 10 spoke perfect, unaccented English and had a sufficient knowledge of slang to pass

SS-Hauptsturmführer Walter Girg. A true daredevil, Girg was so successful in disguising his identity when on operations that at one point he came close to being executed as a traitor by German troops who at first refused to believe that he was a member of Skorzeny's SS-Jagdverbände. (Author's collection)

themselves off as Americans. Many of the brigade's soldiers were capable of nothing more than issuing basic military commands in English, backed up with suitable profanities. An obvious additional problem was that men – often sailors – recruited solely for their linguistic ability had to be given a crash course in communications, demolitions and all the other necessary combat skills.

Even scaled down to two battalions, Skorzeny's command had to incorporate a company from his SS-Jagverband Mitte and two from SS-Fallschirmjäger Bataillon 600. Two battalions of Luftwaffe paratroopers, plus Army troops from a tank, a tank-destroyer, a recce and a signals company were also transferred into PzBde 150, as were artillery gunners, engineers and brigade staff officers. The unit finally numbered around 2,500 men in total, of whom only about 500 were Waffen-SS personnel. They were separated between three battle groups designated Kampfgruppen X, Y and Z (the last two commanded by Army officers), and tasked with seizing the Meuse bridges at Amay, Huy and/or Andenne. The jeep-mounted disguised 'commando' teams (Einheit Stielau) were to blow ammunition dumps and unwanted bridges, remove or change Allied road and minefield signs, spread false information, reconnoitre in depth and radio their findings, and also provide spearhead scouts for conventional units.

On 16 December 1944, the three battlegroups of PzBde 150 went into action in the Ardennes, following immediately behind the lead elements of 1. and 12.SS-Pz Divs and 12.Volks Grenadier Division, with the intention of branching out along side roads as these reached various objectives. In fact initial progress was extremely slow, delayed by very severe traffic congestion on the roads and stiffer enemy resistance than expected. It was immediately clear to Skorzeny that capturing the Meuse bridges was completely impossible. On the night of 17/18 December he sought, and was given, approval for the

Beside the road at Géromont, US Engineers check out an abandoned StuG III assault gun from Kampfgruppe Y, Panzerbrigade 150. The olive drab paint job and Allied white stars do nothing to disguise its silhouette, which is what American troops would have seen some time before they could make out its colour and markings. (US National Archives)

cancellation of that part of Operation *Greif*, and his brigade was reunited and placed at the disposal of I SS-Panzerkorps as a conventional unit.

The brigade's first objective was to seize the key road junction at Malmédy. Earlier intelligence proved outdated, and when Kampfgruppen X and Y launched their attacks on 21 December they ran into unexpectedly strong resistance backed up by heavy artillery fire. The battered Kampfgruppe Y was forced to withdraw almost immediately, and although Kampfgruppe X (led by SS-Hstuf von Fölkersam, the former Brandenburger who had distinguished himself at Maikop) persisted for several hours it too was eventually forced to pull back, von Fölkersam himself being badly wounded. While making his way to the headquarters of 1.SS-Pz Div to report, Skorzeny was hit in the head by artillery splinters and almost blinded. Despite doctors insisting that he be evacuated he refused to leave his men until he was summoned to the Führerhauptquartier to give his report on Operation *Greif*. Despite the failure of the operation, Hitler was pleased with Skorzeny's performance and awarded him the Honour Roll Clasp of the German Army.

Panzerbrigade 150 remained with the 'Leibstandarte' Division until 28 December, when it was withdrawn from the front for transfer back to Grafenwöhr. There it was officially disbanded, and the surviving non-SS troops returned to their original units.

Whilst the bulk of Panzerbrigade 150 failed to achieve their objectives, some of Skorzeny's commando teams did succeed in carrying out their designated tasks. One of the teams reached the bridge at Huy, and managed

Much more convincing is this PzKw V Ausf G Panther disguised with extensive extra plates as an M10 tank-destroyer; note that the hull is seen here from three-quarter front, but the turret is traversed to 'six o'clock'. It was photographed where it came to rest in La Falize village after the 21 December battle for Malmédy, when SS-Hstuf von Fölkersam's Kampfgruppe X were supported by five of these tanks. (US National Archives)

to divert a US armoured column onto a long and pointless detour away from the front line. Other teams succeeded in blocking roads and causing general confusion; one even managed to persuade an American unit busy setting up defensive positions to retreat in order to avoid being cut off by fictitious German movements on their flanks. So great was the American paranoia over the actions of these commandos that many US troops were arrested by their own side on suspicion of being 'German spies', and some firefights broke out between different groups of US soldiers.

Although PzBde 150 were unable to find much in the way of captured Allied armoured vehicles in usable condition they did have a good fleet of functioning jeeps. This one came to grief along with its crew. (US National Archives)

The fate of those members of Skorzeny's 'Einheit Stielau' who were captured is exemplified by one such three-man team – Unteroffizier Pernass, Oberfähnrich Billing and Gefreiter Schmidt. Stopped by a US Military Police checkpoint and unable to give the correct password, they were immediately arrested. Since they were wearing American uniforms, and were in possession of fake identity documents and large sums in US currency, they were tried by court-martial as spies; all were found guilty, and executed by firing squad on 23 December 1944. (It also seems that significant numbers of German soldiers were captured wearing – simply for the sake of warmth – such items as American field jackets, greatcoats and winter overboots in conjunction with their own uniforms. In the atmosphere of 'spy mania' created by Einheit Stielau's real and rumoured activities, they often paid for this booty with their lives.)

US Military Policemen guard two members of Skorzeny's commando who formed part of Operation *Greif*; captured whilst wearing US uniforms, they are doomed to court-martial and execution. Some men of Einheit Stielau were caught in possession of false identity documents and also considerable sums in US currency. (US National Archives)

THE ODER FRONT, 1945

During the final months of the war, Skorzeny was ordered to form a defensive bridgehead at Schwedt on the Oder river, a few miles west of Königsberg. He travelled eastwards from Friedenthal (still using some of the captured American jeeps), and on arrival at Schwedt he found that in additional to his own Jagdverband he would have to face the might of the Red Army with a battalion of pioneers and three grossly under-strength battalions of elderly reservists.

At this time the roads were clogged with civilian refugees fleeing the advancing Soviets, as well as considerable numbers of soldiers from fragmented units trying to make their way westwards. Sending his reconnaissance platoons over onto the east bank of the Order, he ordered his troops to set up positions on the exit roads from Königsberg and escort both civilian and military personnel safely to Kolberg. Here, military personnel were assembled at the local barracks and those who were fit for combat were assigned to Skorzeny's Jagdverband. Though the quality of many of these odds and ends was distinctly variable Skorzeny was happy to have the additional resources. Reinforcements in the form of a regiment of RAD (Labour Corps) troops and a battalion of Volkssturm from Hamburg also arrived, and were put to work straight away helping the pioneers construct defensive fortifications.

The arrival of SS paratroopers, three batteries of Luftwaffe Flak and three companies of surplus Luftwaffe personnel gave Skorzeny a significant boost, as did the discovery of a factory nearby with a stock of 7.5cm anti-tank guns. An outer perimeter was established on the eastern bank of the Oder, and part of Skorzeny's force was despatched to help defend Königsberg. Other reinforcements that gradually filtered through to Skorzeny included a newly-raised and inexperienced battalion from Fallschirmpanzerkorps Hermann Göring and, albeit temporarily, an assault gun detachment sent by Reichsführer-SS Himmler; but there was little chance of Skorzeny being able to hold back the Red Army. Soon advance Soviet units had penetrated Königsberg's defensive rings, and although the troops sent by Skorzeny made a spirited attempt to hold open the links between that city and the bridgehead at Kolberg, Königsberg had been surrounded by late January 1945. (The German defenders were only finally forced to surrender on 9 April.)

Skorzeny's troops continued to defend their bridgehead robustly, launching several local counter-attacks with temporary success, but in the event Skorzeny himself would not see the final events at Kolberg unfold, since he was ordered to return to Berlin on 28 February. There he received orders to transfer the staff element of his Jagdverband to the so-called 'Alpenfestung', the mythical 'Alpine Redoubt'. During a conversation with Hitler in late March, he learned that he was to be awarded the Oakleaves to his Knight's Cross to reward his performance on the Oder front; the award

Henri-Chapelle, 23 December: this fate befell at least 13 and perhaps 18 members of Einheit Stielau. This unfortunate individual is not a Waffen-SS man but a volunteer from the Army, Uffz Manfred Pernass, captured at a checkpoint at Aywaille on 17 December with his comrades Gunther Billing and Wilhelm Schmidt. (During interrogation Schmidt apparently repeated a rumour that Skorzeny's commandos had been ordered to capture Gen Eisenhower.) All three men were tried as spies and executed. (US National Archives)

was officially conferred on 9 April. Skorzeny took no further part in any major military operations, and surrendered to US troops on 20 May 1945.

Skorzeny's reputation led to his immediate arrest, and he was subjected to interrogation over several months regarding his wartime activities, both real and imaginary. When he was taken to Nuremberg as a witness during the trials Allied paranoia over his reputation was reflected in wild rumours of a rescue attempt, leading to increased security precautions. Skorzeny's status changed from witness to accused in July 1947, when he was charged with war crimes in relation to the Ardennes offensive, but all these charges were soon dropped.[1] His captivity now rested solely on his being a former officer in the Waffen-SS, a category subject to immediate arrest.

1 Skorzeny's presence at Malmédy on 21 December led to his being charged on the mistaken assumption that his unit was among those responsible for the shooting of US prisoners at the Baugnez crossroads on 17 December – the 'Malmédy Massacre'. The charges were quietly dropped once it was established that none of Skorzeny's troops had been present. The second count was based on a claim that his men had been ordered to fight while wearing US uniforms, thus violating the laws of war. Skorzeny's commandos were indeed under orders to wear Allied clothing over their German uniforms, but to discard them if capture was imminent. International law clearly differentiates between using enemy guise in order to move around undetected, which is permissible, and actually opening fire on the enemy while dressed in their uniform, which is not. The distinction may be hair-splitting, but as there was no evidence that Skorzeny had issued orders for his men to engage Allied troops while in disguise these charges, too, were dropped.

OTTO SKORZENY

Born in Vienna on 12 June 1908, Skorzeny belonged to a middle-class military family and was fortunate enough to receive a good education, his foreign languages including fluency in both French and English. At university, like many young men of his era, he developed a love of *Mensur* fencing. It is estimated that he took part in at least thirteen duels, one of which resulted in a distinctive scar on his left cheek, which added to the mystique surrounding the man who would become known as 'Scarface Skorzeny'.

Graduating with a degree in engineering (hence the 'dipl. Ing.' in his title) Skorzeny gained work in civil engineering. He developed a sympathy for the Nazi party, joining its Austrian branch in 1931 and becoming a member of the Sturmabteilung (SA). Skorzeny soon moved on from the SA to join the elite SS.

On the outbreak of war, Skorzeny had volunteered for the Luftwaffe only to be rejected as too old at the age of 31. In early 1940 he entered the Waffen-SS, joining the division 'Das Reich' as an officer cadet, and as an engineer he was given the task of ensuring his unit's tanks were kept maintained and operational.

During the invasion of Yugoslavia, a small squad commanded by Skorzeny captured a group of 57 Yugoslavian officers and men, a feat which earned him a field commission. Two months later during Operation *Barbarossa* he was hit in the head by shrapnel, a wound which eventually forced his evacuation to Germany for hospital treatment.

After several months' recuperation, Skorzeny found himself assigned to train soldiers in sabotage, espionage and other special duties. He had been recommended by Ernst Kaltenbrunner, head of the RSHA, whose acquaintance he had made during pre-war days in Vienna.

From then on, Skorzeny would be deeply involved with Germany's special forces and in covert operations on numerous fronts, most successfully with the rescue of Mussolini in 1943, the seizing of the Castle in Budapest in 1944, and – most notoriously, if unsuccessfully – the infiltration of Allied lines by his English-speaking 'Commandos' during the battle of the Bulge.

After the war, the most influential leader of Germany's special-forces troops spent three years

Otto Skorzeny, pictured in captivity. (US National Archives)

in prison awaiting 'de-Nazification'; he was a victim of his own reputation, but all war-crimes charges against him had been dropped for lack of evidence. Never formally released from captivity, Skorzeny was helped to escape on 27 July 1948 (allegedly, by some of his former troops masquerading as US MPs!), and made his way to Spain The mystique surrounding him gave birth to wild rumours of his being behind the so-called 'Odessa' movement which helped suspected SS war criminals to escape, involvement in training Arab military forces in their struggle against Israel, and the elimination of former SS men who were prepared to give evidence against those wanted by the Allies.

In 1970 Skorzeny was diagnosed with a cancerous tumour on the spine. The operation for its removal left him paralysed below the waist, but by sheer strength of will he had learned to walk again within six months. The surgery had only delayed the inevitable however, and on 6 July 1975 he finally succumbed to the disease.

SS PARATROOPERS

SS-Fallschirmjäger Bataillon 500

The origins of the SS-Fallschirmjäger-Bataillon lay in the disciplinary processes within the Waffen-SS, and the concept of Bewährungsschützen – 'disciplinary soldiers' or B-Soldaten. These were men who had committed offences serious enough to warrant trial by court-martial (as opposed to minor offences dealt with within the unit), and who in many cases had been sentenced to either long periods of imprisonment or, in extreme cases, to death. Such sentences were usually carried out at the SS penal camp at Danzig-Matzkau.

In August 1943, Himmler issued an order that up to 600 of these men were to be transferred to a new paratroop unit and given the opportunity to redeem themselves in combat – this despite his having been advised that only a small proportion of them were considered suitable for training as paratroopers. It was originally intended that the new unit would be used primarily on anti-partisan operations, and indeed the unit's first title was SS-Fallschirm Banden-Jäger Bataillon ('SS Parachute Partisan-Hunter Battalion'). However, by the time of the official announcement of the formation of the unit, on 6 September 1943, the title had changed to simply SS-Fallschirmjäger Bataillon.

The men allocated to the battalion were sent to the Luftwaffe's Paratroop School No. 3 at Mataruška Banja to begin their jump training. Not all the personnel were military prisoners; a cadre of regular Waffen-SS combat veterans were also transferred into the unit, some of whom were decidedly unhappy to find themselves serving alongside convicts. The fact that many of the disciplinary cases were indeed unsuitable was confirmed when around 100 of them were returned to the SS authorities, either as being physically unfit or, in some cases, having being caught selling equipment (including weapons) on the black market. After completing their training at the Hungarian airborne base at Papa, to which Fallschirmschule III had relocated, the remaining men of the SS Paratroop Battalion were allocated to anti-partisan duties in Yugoslavia, and during this period the unit was officially renamed as SS-Fallschirmjäger Bataillon 500.

The unit's first real test came during Operation *Maibaum* in April–May 1944 when, under the command of SS-Hstuf Kurt Rybka, it assisted V SS-Gebirgskorps in an operation intended to destroy Tito's 3rd Partisan Corps near Srebrenica in Bosnia. Partisan units attempting to advance into western Serbia were halted by the SS troops and suffered heavy losses.

Almost immediately afterwards the unit began preparing for their next operation, as the Germans prepared to follow up their success with an attack on Tito's own headquarters at Drvar. The plan envisaged various Army and Waffen-SS units converging on the area from north, south, east and west, whilst SS-Fallschirmjäger Bataillon 500 parachuted directly into Drvar. A total of some 280 men, divided into three groups, were to parachute into the immediate area of Tito's headquarters in the hills to the west of Drvar, and attempt to capture the Partisan leader. At the same time a further six groups were to land by glider, with subsidiary targets including the capture of the British, American and Soviet military missions with the Partisans and also the radio station at Drvar.

The operation began in the early morning of 25 May 1944 and almost immediately hit serious problems. Many Fallschirmjäger were injured during landing on the rocky slopes, and the glider-borne element was particularly unlucky, one entire squad being killed when their glider crashed. Rybka himself was seriously wounded by grenade fragments; his troops eventually secured the cave in which Tito's headquarters had been located and the immediate surroundings, but all that they captured was his new dress uniform.

Strong Partisan forces were still in the area, and the SS-Fallschirmjäger found themselves under increasing pressure as their adversaries attempted to recapture the lost ground. Casualties were heavy, but the paratroopers got some support from Stuka dive-bombers and some airdropped ammunition resupply. By the following day troops of 7. SS-Freiwilligen Gebirgs Division 'Prinz Eugen' were arriving, and the Partisan forces were finally forced to withdraw. The survivors of SS-Fallschirmjäger Bataillon 500 remained in the area, carrying out numerous anti-partisan sweeps along with mountain troops from 'Prinz Eugen' before, in June, the battered battalion was withdrawn to Ljubljana for rest and recuperation. Around 850 men from the battalion had taken part in the action at Drvar, of whom only about 250 remained in the ranks.

Command passed to SS-Hstuf Siegfried Milius and work began on rebuilding the unit. Reinforcements arrrived, in the shape of men who had been left out of battle, fresh volunteers and more probationary troops. The problems involved in allocating too many men with bad disciplinary records to what should have been an elite combat unit had been appreciated, and only the 'best' of the B-Soldaten were now posted in. (Others who were

A member of SS-Fallschirmjäger Bataillon 500. Note the use of the standard Luftwaffe paratrooper helmet, without insignia in this case, and a standard splinter-pattern camouflage jump smock complete with its original Luftwaffe breast eagle. Only the SS-pattern belt buckle and the visible SS rank patch on his tunic collar identify his service. (Josef Charita)

Paratroopers from SS-Fallschirmjäger Bataillon 500 on the Eastern Front, with a Sturmgeschutz III in support. They wear a mixture of field-grey Waffen-SS uniforms, Luftwaffe jump smocks and Luftwaffe paratroop helmets. (Josef Charita)

considered 'redeemable' would join Skorzeny's Jagdverband, and the worst of what remained would be sent to the infamous SS-Sonderkommando Dirlewanger. The battalion was subsequently sent to Gotenhafen in East Prussia, from where it had been planned to use the SS-Fallschirmjäger in an operation to the Aaland Islands to block the Gulf of Bothnia. The operation was cancelled, and instead the paratroopers found themselves attached to III (germanische) SS-Panzerkorps under SS-Ogruf Felix Steiner on the Narva front, where some albeit temporary success was achieved in halting several Soviet advances. The battalion were sent to Lithuania in July 1944, and attached to a Kampfgruppe from the elite Panzerkorps 'Grossdeutschland' for an operation to relieve the city of Vilnius. The German force succeeded in penetrating Soviet-held territory, reaching Vilnius and thereafter escorting thousands of cut-off German troops back to the relative safety of German-held territory. Though the battalion suffered only minor losses during this operation, subsequent heavy fighting south-west of Vilnius saw the approximately 260 men who then remained with the battalion reduced to only about 70 survivors. These were transferred to Sakiai, where the unit was to receive around 100 much-needed replacements.

At the end of August 1944 the remnant of the battalion was moved first to East Prussia and then on to Austria, where they were placed at the disposal of Otto Skorzeny. Skorzeny employed them during Operation *Panzerfaust* in Budapest on 15 October, when the SS paratroopers took part in the successful occupation of Castle Hill in Budapest; they infiltrated passages under the castle, and from these into the War and Interior ministries.

SS-Fallschirmjäger Bataillon 600

In fact, on 1 October SS-Fallschirmjäger Bataillon 500 had been officially disbanded, and its survivors became the nucleus of a new unit, SS-Fallschirmjäger Bataillon 600.

The reason for the change was that the '500' number series was typically used for probationary units, and Himmler had decided that he no longer wished the unit to be 'tainted' with the implication of second-rate character. Indeed, the percentage of disciplinary cases within the battalion had decreased

SS PARATROOPS

1: SS-Jäger, SS-Fallschirmjäger Bataillon 500; Bucharest, October 1944
Parading after the successful Operation *Panzerfaust*, this man is identifiable only by his Waffen-SS belt buckle. He wears the Luftwaffe paratroop helmet without insignia; the Luftwaffe second-type jump smock in splinter camouflage pattern, again without insignia; field-grey jump trousers, and front-lacing jump boots. For parade his equipment is reduced to the belt and two sets of triple rifle ammunition pouches, and he presents arms with the Mauser 98k rifle.

2: SS-Sturmann, SS-FJ Btl 500; Memel bend, Baltic front, July 1944
This senior private MG42 gunner also closely resembles an Air Force paratrooper; he is identifiable to his service only by his buckle, and by the fact that the field-grey collar of his M1943 tunic is turned outside his jump smock, exposing the collar patches of service and rank. As the gun 'No.1' he has a holstered Walther P38 pistol for self-protection.

3: SS-Oberscharführer, SS-FJ Btl 600; Eastern Front, November 1944
This figure is based on a photo of the decorated senior NCO Walter Hummel (see page 44) wearing M1936-style service dress, complete with the enlisted ranks' service cap with infantry-white piping. His status as a paratrooper is shown by his bloused trousers and jump boots, and the Luftwaffe Paratrooper Badge on his left pocket. His other awards are the Iron Cross 1st Class, the Wound Badge in Silver and the Infantry Assault Badge, and his buttonhole-ribbons are those of the Iron Cross 2nd Class over the *Ostmedaille* for the Russian winter campaign of 1941/42. Apart from the odd use of an Army Panzer-pattern breast eagle in place of the SS sleeve eagle, the most noticeable thing about Hummel's insignia is the continued display of the distinctions of his former unit – the 'D' shoulder strap cipher and 'Deutschland' cuff title of that regiment of the 'Das Reich' Division. This was normal practice among combat veterans who transferred into the parachute battalion from other units, as opposed to military convicts.

by now from around 70 per cent to 30 per cent, and even these were considered the most promising of the potential material. Recruits were by now mostly regular personnel rather than military convicts, including men from the Army and Kriegsmarine as well as the Waffen-SS, and by November unit strength was back up to just under 700 men.

The battalion's association with Skorzeny was made permanent on 10 November, when SS-Fallschirmjäger Bataillon 600 was formally absorbed into the SS-Jagdverbände. At the end of January 1945 the unit formed part of Skorzeny's force for the defensive bridgehead at Schwedt on the Oder; the paratroopers were positioned in the Königsberg area, operating with SS-Jagdverband Mitte around Grabow. There, on 4 February, its 3. Kompanie was completely overrun by the Soviets, suffering heavy casualties; the survivors took part in efforts to retake the city a few days later, but after some initial progress the battered German formations were once again forced out of Königsberg. The battalion's defensive positions around Grabow came under repeated attack by Soviet armour, and many tanks fell victim to the Panzerfausts of the SS paratroopers.

It was decided that SS-Fallschirmjäger Bataillon 600 and SS-Jagdverband Mitte were to be temporarily merged to form an SS regiment, which would be held as the reserve for Skorzeny's Schwedt bridgehead. Shortly afterwards, however, Hitler decided that the defenders of the bridgehead could be withdrawn. SS-Fallschirmjäger Bataillon 600 was then moved southwards to another east-bank bridgehead at Zehenden to the south-west of Königsberg. Here, on 6 March, in its merged form with Jagdverband Mitte, the battalion joined a number of other smaller Waffen-SS units in a new SS-Kampfgruppe Solar, which came under the control of the newly formed Division zbV 610 (Special Duties Division 610) – by now, of course, the term 'division' was purely nominal.

On the evening of the same day a stray Soviet artillery shell hit an explosive charge on the bridge over the Oder near Alt-Cüstrinchen which had been prepared for demolition. The bridge was destroyed, effectively cutting off the SS-Fallschirmjäger on the east bank as the Red Army approached. The next two weeks passed quietly enough, but on 25 March a new Soviet offensive began. For two days the SS troops held out against overwhelmingly superior opposition, but on the third day, after sustaining huge losses, they were forced to withdraw. Due to the loss of the bridge the troops were forced to swim the Oder, many being lost to drowning or enemy fire.

In the weeks that followed, the battalion was yet again reinforced and brought up to a respectable strength of well over 800 men. In mid-April 1945 the unit was absorbed into a new SS-Kampfgruppe Harzer, in which it temporarily became part of SS-Polizei PzGren Regt 7, assigned

SS-Oberscharführer Walther Hummel from SS-Fallschirmjäger Bataillon 600. As was typical for experienced combat veterans who transferred to the battalion, Hummel continued to wear the insignia of his previous unit; note on his shoulder strap the 'D' cipher of the 'Deutschland' Standarte. On his breast pocket he wears the Luftwaffe Paratrooper Badge. (Hummel)

to the bridgehead around Eberswalde north-east of Berlin. This was intended to threaten the flank of the advancing Soviets, but the Red Army's advance was so fast and powerful that the proposed attack was cancelled. In late April the battalion found itself assigned to XXXVI Panzerkorps in the defence of the area around Prenzlau, among German units by now at only around 10 per cent of their nominal strength.

The battalion was pushed back to positions west of Fürstenwerder and then to Neubrandenburg, where on 28 April it was involved in heavy defensive fighting before withdrawing west in an effort to avoid Soviet captivity. The remnants of the unit were under constant attack as they withdrew westwards; in one engagement with Soviet horsed cavalry at Neuruppin, the 400 or so SS-Fallschirmjäger who engaged the enemy suffered more than 50 per cent losses. The survivors, numbering fewer than 200 men, surrendered to US forces at Hagenow on 2 May 1945.

THE KRIEGSMARINE

It was not until the liberation of continental Europe by Anglo-American forces was imminent that the Kriegsmarine finally decide to undertake serious development of special naval forces that might be employed to oppose seaborne elements of the invasion. This new branch of the Navy was to be known as the Kleinkampfmittelverbände (literally, 'small battle units'), usually abbreviated to K-Verbände. From 20 April 1944, the Befehlshaber der K-Verbände would be Konteradmiral Helmuth Heye.

Admiral Hellmuth Heye , commander of Germany's Kleinkampfmittelverbände. A career officer since World War I, Heye had served as captain of the heavy cruiser *Admiral Hipper*. (Deutsches U-Boot Museum)

Hellmuth Heye was born in 1895 in Beckingen; he joined the Kaiserliche Marine in 1914 and was commissioned Leutnant zur See in July 1916. He remained in the Navy after the war, and by the outbreak of World War II he had risen through the ranks to Kapitän zur See and was commanding the heavy cruiser *Admiral Hipper*. Heye was in command when the cruiser encountered the British destroyer HMS *Glowworm* during the invasion of Norway; Heye was so impressed by the gallantry of the British sailors in this uneven contest that he sent a message to the British Admiralty via the International Red Cross praising the conduct of his enemy. This chivalrous act contributed to the commander of the destroyer, LtCdr Roope, being awarded a posthumous Victoria Cross. Heye himself would be awarded the Knight's Cross in January 1941 for his period commanding the *Admiral Hipper*. From September 1940 until September 1942, Heye served as chief-of-staff to various naval commands before being promoted to Konteradmiral and appointed as Commanding Admiral for the Black Sea area. He was the personal choice of Grossadmiral Dönitz to command the K-Verbände in April 1944.

Heye wanted only the best manpower that the Kriegsmarine could offer, and chose as his chief-of-staff a highly decorated U-boat ace, Fregattenkapitän Fritz Frauenheim. Frauenheim, a Knight's Cross holder since 29 August 1940, had commanded U-101 with considerable success, sinking 19 vessels during his operational career. He then moved on to command 29. Unterseebootsflottille, before transferring to the K-Verbände. Amongst Heye's other staff officers were Fregattenkapitän Albrecht Brandi, former commander of U-617 and one of only two Navy men to be decorated with the Knight's Cross with Oakleaves, Swords and Diamonds; and Knight's Cross holder Korvettenkapitän Hans Bartels. Bartels had been responsible for building a flotilla of small coastal craft into an effective minesweeping and coastal protection unit which he christened the 'Tigerverband', and on joining the K-Verbände he was responsible for developing the 'Biber' midget submarine.

Given exceptional powers by Dönitz, Heye set about creating his new formation at Heiligenhafen, built around a small cadre of around 30 hand-picked officers and men, all of whom were enthusiastic volunteers. At this point known as the Marine Einsatz Abteilung (Naval Action Detachment), it grew over the next few weeks to number about 150 officers and men.

A 'Biber' type one-man submarine. One of the better designs, technically if not in terms of combat success, it weighed just over 6 tons, could carry two torpedoes and had a decent range. It was used throughout the coastal waters of German-occupied Europe. (Deutsches U-Boot Museum)

Training was carried out under conditions of total secrecy, including instruction from – amongst others – special forces troops from the Army's Brandenburgers. As well as training in the use of the new weapons, instruction was given in escape and evasion and in languages, particularly English.

The standards were extremely high, being comparable with those demanded of, for example, the British Commandos, SAS or SBS; any trainee who failed was returned to his unit, after warnings of the severe consequences of speaking about their experiences or even admitting the existence of the new organization. As in other elite units, however, though the training was tough,

G **SS PARATROOP MORTAR CREW**
This plate recreates the appearance of a three-man mortar team from SS-FJ Btl 500 on the Baltic front in summer 1944. The 8cm schwere Granatwerfer 34 fired 3.5kg (7.7lb) high explosive or smoke projectiles out to ranges of about 2,600 yards, and a practised crew could average some 15 rounds per minute – if the available ammunition held out. The loader (**1**) wears, again, the splinter-pattern Luftwaffe 'bone-sack', this time complete with the Air Force breast eagle. The mortar gunner (**2**) has not bothered to remove the factory-applied Luftwaffe decal from his helmet. He has received an issue of the new Waffen-SS two-piece 'pea

pattern' combat fatigue uniform introduced from March 1944; no insignia were authorized for wear on the four-pocket tunic other than the SS sleeve eagle and the February 1943 system of stylized sleeve rank patches, and the latter are rarely seen in photos of enlisted ranks. The team leader (**3**) has discarded his jump smock but retains the field-grey jump trousers and jump boots, with his standard field-grey service tunic. The collar shows the *Tresse* braid of senior NCO status and the left collar patch of his rank, SS-Scharführer; again, he displays a shoulder-strap cipher and cuff title from his previous unit, in this case the 'Germania' Standarte of the 'Das Reich' Division.

The 12-ton 'Hecht' two-man midget submarine, carrying only one torpedo and with a limited range, was rejected for operational service after a few prototypes were built. These were subsequently used only for training crews for the K-Verbände. (Deutsches U-Boot Museum)

the life Spartan and self-discipline very demanding, most normal 'bureaucratic' discipline was greatly relaxed; all ranks were encouraged to see each other as comrades and equals, each willing to trust his life to his fellow 'K-Mann'.

The principal combat elements of the K-Verbände were termed Lehrkommandos, sub-divided into Flotillen. The Lehrkommandos were numbered as follows, with the Flotillen within each Kommando following the same numerical sequence.

THE LEHRKOMMANDOS

Lehrkommando 200
Commanders: Klt Ulrich Kolbe (ex S-boats) April–July 1944; Klt Helmut Bastian (ex U-boats) July 1944–May 1945. Based first at Priesterbeck and then at Plön, this unit operated 'Linsen' speedboats, and was responsible for training operators for K-Flotillen 211 to 220.

The Linsen were known as Sprengboote or 'explosive boats', and about 1,200 were built. Small speedboats just under 6m (19ft 7in) long and weighing just over 1.2 tonnes, they were powered by a 3.6-litre V8 engine giving them a top speed of around 30 knots. The stern of the boat was packed with up to 480kg (1056lb) of explosives, connected to a detonator in the bow. Each attack would be carried out by one command boat and two ramming boats; the pilot would aim the boat at the target and jump overboard at the last safe moment, allowing the boat to be guided into its target by radio control from the command boat. The detonator was timed to allow the boat a few seconds after impact to sink well below the waterline of the target ship's hull before the explosives detonated. The two pilots who had jumped overboard would then (in theory) be picked up by the command boat, which would escape at speed under cover of a smoke screen. Each Linsen Flotille consisted of four Gruppen, with eight Linsen and four command boats.

On 2 August 1944, Linsen from K-Flotille 211 attacked and sank landing ship LCG 764 and a tanker off the Normandy coast; this attack also involved E-boats and 'Marder' one-man torpedoes. While the ram-boats themselves were obviously expendable, two command boats and eight men were also lost in this operation.

The 'Molch' type one-man midget submarine used by Lehrkommando 400 was the least successful of several designs. Although nearly 400 were built, when it was committed to operations in the coastal waters of the Mediterranean and the North Sea the flotillas suffered catastrophic casualty rates without achieving any combat success. (Deutsches U-Boot Museum)

During a further attack on 8 August, again with E-boats in support, an Allied minesweeper, a freighter and a workshop ship were sunk for the loss of four German crewmen. (Where Linsen were operating in combination with other vessels it was often difficult to determine with absolute certainty whether targets were hit by a Linsen, a torpedo fired by a Marder or one fired by an E-boat.) Operations off the Belgian and Dutch coasts from late 1944 onwards also scored some minor successes; on 31 October 1944 a troopship, a freighter loaded with munitions, an anti-aircraft lighter and a searchlight barge were sunk. One small success was also scored on 17 April 1945, when Linsen succeeded in penetrating the Allied blockade of the port of Dunkirk and brought much-needed food and munitions to the beleaguered German garrison.

August 1944 also saw attacks by Linsen on Allied shipping in the Mediterranean and Adriatic, but with very little success; many of the speedboats were destroyed by Allied air raids, intercepted by Allied warships or lost in heavy seas. The only notable success was the sinking of the French destroyer *Trombe* on 17 April 1945.

Lehrkommando 250

Commander: Kkp Hans Bartels, August 1944–May 1945. Based at Lübeck; responsible for training crews for 'Biber' midget submersibles and controlling K-Flotillen 261 to 270.

The Biber (Beaver) was a small one-man submersible (i.e. not a true submarine) just 9m long (29ft 6in) and weighing some 6.5 tons, powered by a small petrol engine as used in Opel trucks, and carrying two torpedoes slung externally along the lower hull sides. The boat was capable of diving to depths of up to 60m (197ft), but could only launch torpedoes when on the surface, and its poor sea-going qualities made a successful attack in any but the calmest seas impossible. Additionally, if the pilot submerged the vessel for too long he was in danger of being asphyxiated by carbon-monoxide fumes from the engine's exhaust (a number of pilots were lost in this way when on operations).

A 'Neger' type one-man torpedo; this gives a good impression of just how little of the vessel was visible once it was at sea. Note the flimsy Plexiglas dome that was the pilot's only protection from the elements and the enemy. The vertical line just in front of this is the aiming-post that he was supposed to line up with the target before launching the torpedo. (Deutsches U-Boot Museum)

By the time the Biber was ready for operational use in August 1944 many of its intended base ports had been taken by the Allies; several boats were also lost, and pilots killed, during air attacks and contact with Allied ground forces while on their way to the front. On 22 December 1944 a Biber succeeded in torpedoing and sinking the munitions ship *Alan-a-Dale*, but this was to be the type's only confirmed success. Most Biber operations were a catalogue of disasters, with boats sunk by warships, aircraft, heavy seas or the poisoning of the pilot.

Lehrkommando 300

Commanders (all ex U-boats): Lt Kiep, June–July 1944; Klt Hermann Rasch, July 1944–February 1945; Fkp Albrecht Brandi, February–May 1945. Based at Neustadt; responsible for training crews for 'Hecht' and 'Seehund' midget submarines and controlling K-Flotillen 311 to 316.

The Hecht (Pike) was an electrically powered submersible 10.4m (34ft 1in) in length and weighing 12 tons. With a two-man crew, it was capable of diving to around 50m (164ft), and carried a single torpedo or mine. However, it had poor sea-going qualities, and in the event only three were built and used for training.

The Seehund (Seal) was a true two-man midget submarine, and was in fact given a U-boat type designation as the Type XXVII. Some 12m (39ft 4in) long and displacing 15 tons, it was powered by a diesel engine capable of expelling exhaust gases underwater to a depth of 20m (65ft 7in), so the diesel engine could be used when submerged. It carried two torpedoes externally and could dive to 30m (98ft 5 inches).

The first operation involving 18 Seehunde was launched on 1 January 1945, but the only victim was a British trawler sunk on the following day; one Seehund hit a mine and sank, and 15 others were sunk by Allied action. A second operation on 12 January involved just four boats, two of which were forced to abort due to technical problems and Allied activity; the remaining two returned safely after sinking a collier in the Thames Estuary. Several more operations followed, without success but with several boats lost. The next successes were achieved in late February: on the 22nd the tank landing ship LST 364 was sunk, the following day the French destroyer *La Combattante*, and on the 26th two freighters, the *Rampant* and the *Nashaba*. More importantly, during 33 operations launched during that month only four Seehunde were lost, as the crews gained both confidence and experience. On 21 March a large munitions ship was torpedoed and sunk by a Seehund. As the war drew to a close fuel shortages seriously curtailed operations, but despite this Seehunde sank the tanker Y17, the freighter *Samida*, the cable-layer *Monarch*, the

This shot shows to advantage the tiny, cramped cockpit of the Neger, and the pilot's cloth flying-type helmet. (Deutsches U-Boot Museum)

freighters *Benjamin H. Bristow* and *Svere Helmersen*. A number of other ships were damaged by torpedoes including the destroyer HMS *Puffin*, which was eventually written off after being rammed by a Seehund whose torpedo then exploded. Although the Seehund operations could never claim really significant results, the fact that they sunk a total of some 120,000 tons of Allied shipping is a testament to the bravery of the sailors who crewed these boats under the most difficult of circumstances.

The Neger pilot Oberschreibermaat Walter Gerhold is congratulated by Grossadmiral Dönitz on the award of his Knight's Cross. This decoration recognized Gerhold's success in torpedoing the Polish destroyer *Dragon* off Normandy on 7 July 1944; the warship was so badly damaged it was abandoned the following day. (Deutsches U-Boot Museum)

Lehrkommando 350

Commanders: Klt Heinz Franke, July 1944–March 1945; Klt Horst Kessler, March–May 1945. Based at Surendorf; responsible for training crews for 'Neger' and 'Marder' one-man torpedoes and controlling K-Flotillen 361 to 366.

Unlike the midget submersible types, the Neger and Marder can more accurately be described as manned torpedoes. The design consisted of two torpedoes, one above the other; the upper had the warhead replaced by a tiny cockpit with a domed plexiglass cover, the lower retained a live warhead. The rather unfortunately titled Neger (Nigger) was a play on the name of the creator, Richard Mohr (Mohr – Moor or Blackamoor). The Marder (Marten) was an improved version almost identical in appearance, but slightly longer and with the capability to dive to around 10m (33ft). Neither was particularly effective, with a loss rate of up to 80 per cent, but some successes were achieved.

The Neger were first used in an attack on the Allied-occupied port at Anzio on 20 April 1944; three ships were sunk and a number of harbour installations destroyed. The next use was in Normandy, where on 5 July 1944 a total of 26 Neger were launched against Allied shipping; a number of the

The tower of a 'Seehund' type midget submarine or 'Type XXVII U-boat', the biggest and most successful of the small submarines, which was used by Lehrkommando 300. Note the attempt at camouflage, with dabs of light-coloured paint mottled over the basic dark grey scheme. At least 1,000 of these 15-ton vessels were planned, but only around 300 were constructed before the war ended. In February–March 1945 Seehund crews sank about 120,000 tons of Allied shipping including several warships. (Deutsches U-Boot Museum)

pilots on this occasion were actually members of Skorzeny's SS-Jagdverbände. HMS *Trollope* was struck by a torpedo from a Neger piloted by Walter Gerhold – often erroneously attributed to an E-boat – and the minesweepers HMS *Cato* and *Magic* were sunk. Two days later the Polish destroyer *Dragon* and the minesweeper HMS *Plyades* also fell victim to Negers. Losses were unacceptably high, however, and this was to be the last Neger operation on the invasion front. Operations by the Marder version from 14–16 August 1944 sank an ammunition ship and the destroyer HMS *Isis* and damaged other ships, but once again only at the cost of heavy losses.

Subsequent attempts to use Marders in the Mediterranean were singularly unsuccessful, with heavy losses sustained and no Allied vessels sunk.

Lehrkommando 400

Commanders: Klt Heinz Franke, July 1944–March 1945; Klt Horst Kessler, March-May 1945. Based at Surendorf alongside Lehrkommando 350 and with the same commanders; responsible for training crews for the 'Molch' midget submarine and controlling K-Flotillen 411 to 417.

The Molch (Salamander) was a one-man submersible torpedo-carrier some 11m (36ft) long and displacing 11 tons; powered by an electric motor, it carried two torpedoes externally. Rushed into service before being properly trialled, the Molch was a disaster. On their first operational use, in the Mediterranean on 25 September 1944, of 12 that set out ten were lost. On 22 February 1945, during an operation in the Scheldt, of ten that set out six failed to return. Finally, an operation on 12 March saw 14 lost out of the 16 that set out. No Allied vessel ever fell victim to a Molch.

Lehrkommando 600

Commander: Klt Heinz Schomberg, October 1944–May 1945. Responsible for training crews of assault boats (Sturmboote), and for controlling K-Flotillen 611 to 615.

This interesting shot of Seehund crew members shows the black leather clothing, including a jacket whose cut closely resembled that of the special black uniform for tank crews. (Deutsches U-Boot Museum)

K-Verbände units saw heavy action in the Adriatic, where they used various assault boats to effect landings behind Allied lines to carry out acts of sabotage or attack installations. Larger assault boats were also used against enemy shipping and port installations. Few personnel survived; many of those who were captured were murdered by partisans, and the combat records of the K-Flotillen involved were lost or destroyed.

Lehrkommando 700

Commanders: Marineståbsarzt Dr Wandel, June 1944–Jan 1945; KKp Hermann Ludtke, January–May 1945. Located initially in Venice and later on the German island of Sylt; responsible for training combat frogmen and controlling K-Flotillen 702 and 704.

The earliest German unit of combat frogmen was created around a cadre of volunteers, principally from the Brandenburg's Küstenjäger but also including men from the Abwehr and the SD. Amongst other places, training was undertaken in secret at the SS-Junkerschule at Bad Tölz in Bavaria. Controlled by Skorzeny's SS-Jagdverbände organization, frogmen were often employed for sabotage work, and might be considered as equivalent to the modern SBS or US Navy SEALs; as well as being super-fit and proficient divers, they were trained in unarmed combat, sniping, demolition work, radio communications, driving numerous types of vehicle, and foreign languages.

Their first significant operations came in June 1944, when frogmen towed torpedo-shaped containers full of explosives along the river Orne through Allied lines in Normandy, and secured them to bridge supports; both later successfully detonated by automatic timers. On 26 August 1944, frogmen were landed near Le Havre by Linsen speedboats from the K-Verbände, evaded Allied sentries and sneaked into a captured coastal artillery emplacement whose guns had been turned to attack the German garrison; they successfully placed demolition charges which destroyed the battery.

A further successful raid took place on 15 September 1944, when frogmen landed from Linsen speedboats succeeded in demolishing the lock gate at Kruisschans in Allied-occupied Antwerp. An attempt on the bridges over the Waal at Nijmegen was successful in that frogmen succeeded in reaching the bridge and attaching their explosives, which detonated, but proved to be inadequate to destroy the bridge. Now fully alerted, the Allies were able to foil subsequent attempts to finish the job.

In the closing stages of the war combat frogmen, often working in conjunction with Linsen, were active on the Eastern Front, predominantly in attacks on bridges with the intention of slowing the Soviet advance. Bridges at Eisenhüttenstadt, Kalenzig, Rebus, Zellin, Dievenow, Nipperweise and Fiddichow were destroyed or put out of action by units of the K-Verbände.

Though few in number and only raised in the last year of the war, the men of the K-Verbände displayed exceptional bravery. Although sent on many

No distinctive uniform was issued to the members of the K-Verbände, but this special black leather clothing seems to have been worn only rarely by sailors other than members of this branch. (Deutsches U-Boot Museum)

so-called 'Himmelfahrtskommandos' or virtual suicide missions, the K-Männer never entered combat with anything other than a determination to succeed and survive.

Special clothing and insignia

No uniforms were designed specifically for the men of the K-Verbände, but they did wear some rather interesting items rarely seen in more conventional naval units.

Sprengboot crews were issued with the Luftwaffe's standard paratrooper's jump helmet. K-Verbände personnel might also be seen wearing a black leather outfit. The trousers were the standard issue worn widely within the Navy, particularly by engineroom crews. The jacket, however, was a rather stylish waist-length, double-breasted garment bearing a close resemblance in cut to the black uniform jacket worn by Panzer crewmen.

A special insignia series, known as the Kampfabzeichen der Kleinkampfmittelverbände, was created in order to recognize the bravery and determination of the men of the K-Verbände. On 30 November 1944, Grossadmiral Dönitz instituted the new awards, in seven grades as follows:

1st Grade Embroidered yellow thread swordfish over a circle of rope, all on a circular blue woollen patch.
2nd, 3rd & 4th Grades As 1st, with addition of one, two and three swords.
5th, 6th & 7th Grades Bronze, silver and gold metal clasps.

There was also a 'probationary' level of this award, with a plain swordfish motif without the rope circle. Grade 1 was awarded for some minor act of

Given that little if any of their time was spent on conventional vessels, it is not surprising that in surviving photos of K-Verbände personnel their predominant uniform, apart from the leather clothing, is the field-grey naval land service uniform as worn by this Leutnant. (Deutsches U-Boot Museum)

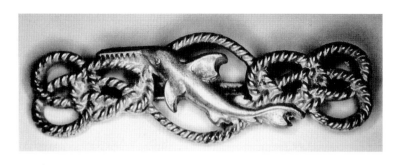

merit, e.g. planning a successful operation. Grade 2 was awarded for participation in a single action, either solo or as a member of a team. Grades 3, 4 and 5 were awarded after taking part in second, third and fourth operations; Grade 6 marked participation in seven operations, and Grade 7 in ten or more.

ABOVE
An extremely rare original example of the metal clasp for Grade 6 of the K-Verbände award. Unusually for awards produced before the war's end, none of the grades in this series featured the swastika in the design. Note the smooth fins on the swordfish; the examples produced post-war as part of the newly approved 'de-Nazified' series of World War II awards had ribbed fins. (Detlev Niemann)

BELOW
An illustration of the cloth sleeve patch for Grade 4 of the special award for operational members of the K-Verbände, awarded after participation in three operations and worn on the right sleeve. (From author's collection)

The insignia of 1st to 4th Grades were to be worn on the upper right sleeve, and the metal clasps on the left breast above the pocket and any ribbon bar. It is known from entries in original paybooks that awards of the lower grades were made, but very late in the war; there were, however, no known awards of the metal clasps.

THE LUFTWAFFE

The German Air Force's involvement in covert and special operations is perhaps the least well known among the armed services.

The principal unit involved was Kampfgeschwader 200. The aura of secrecy surrounding this conventionally titled 'bomber wing' was such that even sub-units within it were not necessarily aware of each others' existence. The destruction and loss of most of the records relating to it – either deliberately or due to Allied action – has only served to compound the sense of mystery surrounding its wartime exploits.

Kampfgeschwader 200 was created on 20 February 1944, following an order issued by the Oberkommando der Luftwaffe. The core around which it was formed was an existing organization, the Versuchsverband Oberbefehlshaber der Luftwaffe ('Air Force Commander-in-Chief's Research Unit'). Previously this had been used to evaluate both new German and captured enemy aircraft, as well as being involved in clandestine intelligence-gathering operations and the insertion of Abwehr personnel behind Allied lines. On March 1944 it was absorbed into the newly formed KG 200, whose formal chain of command led through Luftflotte Reich. The Kampfgeschwader was initially under the command of Obst Heinz Heigl, who was succeeded in this post by Obstlt Werner Baumbach on 15 November 1944.

Baumbach was born at Cloppenburg in 1916. At the age of 19 he joined the new Luftwaffe and trained as a pilot; by the outbreak of war he had gained his commission as a Leutnant and was flying the Heinkel He111 bomber with Kampfgeschwader 30. An attack on a Polish air base in September 1939 gained Baumbach the Iron Cross 2nd Class, and shortly afterwards his 'Adler Geschwader' was re-equipped with the aircraft in which Baumbach was to gain the reputation of an 'expert', the Junkers Ju88 twin-engined dive-bomber. Flying successful anti-shipping operations during the 1940 Western campaign, Baumbach was awarded the Iron Cross 1st Class on 4 May specifically for sinking the French cruiser *Emile Bertin*; this was followed just four days later by the announcement of his Knight's Cross, the first such award to a bomber pilot. Promotion to Oberleutnant followed, and with it an appointment as Staffelkapitän of 1./KG 30.

Operating from bases in northern Norway, Baumbach flew strike missions against Allied convoys and against the UK mainland, and on 14 July 1941 the Oakleaves were added to his Knight's Cross after his record of enemy shipping sunk exceeded 200,000 tons. In July 1942, Baumbach was promoted to Hauptmann and appointed Gruppenkommandeur of I./KG 30. Subsequent operations in the Mediterranean and in the waters around the Crimea saw his tally of shipping sunk rise to an incredible 300,000 tons, an achievement for which he was awarded the Swords to his Oakleaves on 17 August 1942; promotion to Major followed just two months later. After flying his 200th mission Baumbach was withdrawn from combat flying duties.

* * *

The inclusion of already existing elements such as the Versuchsverband meant that within just five months of the order for its creation KG 200 already had access to 32 different aircraft types, both German and captured Allied, and had over 100 trained aircrew. The panel on page 59 shows the location and tasking of the Gruppen and Staffeln.

Covert work undertaken by KG 200 principally involved dropping German agents behind Allied lines. For this purpose a number of B-17 Flying Fortresses were available – it has been estimated that as many as 40 fell into German hands in either airworthy or repairable condition – with a smaller number of B-24 Liberators. (While both Germany and the Allies developed special containers to drop munitions to troops on the ground, and to resistance groups in occupied Europe, the Germans actually developed a large bomb-shaped container to drop the agents themselves. Known as the Personenabwurfgerät or PAG, this could accommodate up to three agents with all their equipment, and had a special foam-filled base to absorb impact when it hit the ground. The practical test results are unknown.)

In addition to dropping agents, less successful attempts were made to use captured B-17s on combat operations. One B-17 was used to drop supplies to the cut-off German garrison in Brest. Supposedly, an attempt (or at least a suggestion) was made to use another to infiltrate a formation of US bombers with the intention of shooting them down as they came in to land. A moment's reflection on the practical difficulties and limited probable dividends makes this seem highly unlikely, and also pointlessly wasteful of a valuable asset. Air-to-air shadowing of US daylight bomber formations, for the purpose of vectoring Luftwaffe interceptors, was a more sensible use for captured bombers.

A number of Allied fighters including Spitfires, P-51 Mustangs and P-47 Thunderbolts were also captured and 'recycled'. After the obvious first step of test-flying them to familiarize Luftwaffe aircrew with their combat

The special awards seem rarely to have been actually presented before the end of the war, most being made 'on paper' only. This award document for the 'Probationary' class was dated on 10 May 1945, two days after the war ended. (Kay Brueggermann)

characteristics such prizes were often handed over to KG 200. The heavy bombers – a category in which the Allies were well ahead of German designers – were particularly valuable in enabling the Luftwaffe to develop attack tactics for their fighter pilots. For operations on the Eastern Front a large number of Petlyakov Pe-2 and Tupolev SB-2 were available; so many of both types had been captured in the opening stages of Operation *Barbarossa* that the Germans were also able to sell significant numbers to their allies.

One rather bizarre-looking aircraft that saw combat service and some limited success with KG 200 was the *Mistel* combination. The concept was that war-weary Junkers Ju88 bombers would be put to good use by fitting a large warhead in the nose and crashing them into their target. To deliver this 'flying bomb', a special cradle and control linkages were built on top of the Junkers, in which a single-engined fighter would be mounted 'piggy-back' fashion. The fighter pilot would remotely control the bomber, and when the target area was reached he would release the Junkers to crash into its target. It was estimated that the shaped warhead would be sufficient to penetrate 8m (26ft) of steel or 20m (65ft) of reinforced concrete.

On 24 June 1944 *Mistels* carried out a successful attack on Allied shipping in the bay of the Seine, sinking several vessels as block-ships. On 6 March 1945, *Mistels* of KG 200 launched an attack on the bridges over the Oder at Goeritz. Already damaged in an attack using Henschel Hs293 guided bombs (see below), two bridges were destroyed by the *Mistels*. A further operation planned for early 1945 might have had a serious, if temporary effect on the Soviet war effort had it succeeded; this involved a massed *Mistel* attack on power-generating plants near Moscow

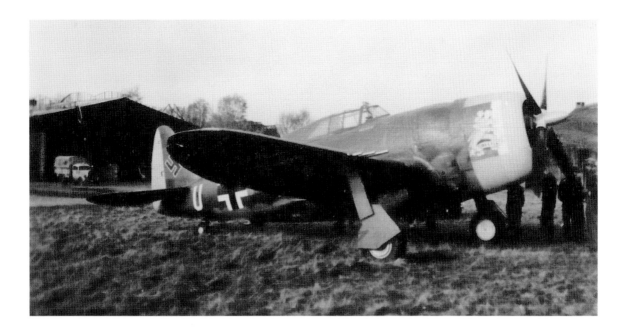

which, it was estimated, supplied almost 80 per cent of the power supply of the Soviet armaments industry. This Operation 'Iron Hammer' came to nothing when the *Mistels* were caught on the ground during a US daylight bombing raid and most of them were destroyed.

One advanced weapon successfully employed by KG 200 was the Henschel Hs293 radio-guided bomb. Essentially a tiny aircraft with short, stubby wings, this had a small rocket motor mounted underneath the fuselage which provided a short but powerful burst of acceleration on being launched from the parent aircraft. Keeping his eye on a bright tail-flare, an operator in the nose of the aircraft attempted to steer the missile towards the target, carrying just under 300kg (660lb) of high explosive. The corvette HMS *Egret* was sunk by 2./KG 200 in the Bay of Biscay on 25 August 1943 using the Hs293 launched from Dornier Do217 aircraft. KG 200 also took part, along with KG 100, in the use of Hs293s launched from the long-range Heinkel He177 (some success was also achieved by He177s of II/KG 40 at Anzio in January 1944). A further operation by KG 200 on 6 March 1945 saw Hs293s being used against the bridge over the Oder at Goeritz, causing damage; the bridge was finally finished off in the *Mistel* attack mentioned above.

Amongst the most unusual aircraft allocated to IV/ KG 200 was the Fieseler Fi103 Reichenberg – in fact, the manned version of the V1 'flying bomb', designed to be carried under the wing of a Heinkel He111 bomber. At a suitable moment the Reichenberg would be released and guided to its destination by the pilot, who would then bale out at the last possible moment. Needless to say, the chances of surviving a bale-out from an inherently unstable aircraft, with a large pulse-jet engine above the fuselage, in a 500mph dive, would have been vanishingly small. Nevertheless, KG 200 had at

A captured USAAF P-47 Thunderbolt bearing the markings of its new owners. After repair, testing, and evaluation by service pilots a number of such captured aircraft found their way to KG 200 for potential use in covert operations. (Thomas Huss)

Kampfgeschwader 200, 1944		
Stab KG 200	Berlin	
I/ KG 200	Finow	
1./KG 200	Finow	Long range operations
2./KG 200	Finow	Short / medium range operations
3./KG 200	Rügen/Flensburg	Maritime operations
4./KG 200	Finow	Training
II/ KG 200	Burg	
5./ KG 200	Burg	Pathfinders & radar jamming
6./ KG 200	Rechlin	*Mistel* operations
7./ KG 200	Rechlin	*Mistel* training
III/ KG 200	Berlin-Stacken	Torpedo-armed Fw190s
IV/ KG 200	Prenzlau	Manned V1 rockets

A captured RAF Wellington medium bomber; such aircraft were often used by KG 200 for making nighttime drops of agents behind Allied lines. (Thomas Huss)

least 100 trained pilots ready for operations, and almost 200 of the flying bombs available. Despite interference from the SS in the person of Otto Skorzeny, who wished the manned V1 to be put into operational use, Obstlt Baumbach enlisted Albert Speer's support in persuading Hitler to finally reject plans for its use, and the potential pilots for these suicide missions were reassigned.

Another advanced aircraft that served experimentally with KG 200 was the Junkers Ju390, a huge four-engined design with the phenomenal range of around 3,700 miles. A special six-engined version which KG 200 also obtained had an even longer range, and is alleged to have made a test flight in 1944 which reached to within 12 miles of the eastern seaboard of the USA. According to the former armaments minister Albert Speer, the Ju390 had also made a non-stop flight from Germany to Japan by flying northwards over the Pole rather than west to east over Soviet territory.

Certainly one of the most audacious – not to say hare-brained – operations with which KG 200 was involved was Operation *Zeppelin* in September 1944. A brainchild of the RSHA, this plan required an aircraft from KG 200 to land close to Moscow and deliver a team of two assassins, one male and one female (both of whom were former Soviet officers), who would then make their way into the city equipped with money and fake documents which, it was believed, would allow them access to the Kremlin, where they would assassinate Stalin. An advance reconnaissance party was parachuted into position and reported back giving the all clear for the operation. An Arado Ar232 from KG 200 carrying the assassins did take off from Riga in Latvia and penetrate Soviet territory, but came under fire as it approached the landing site. The original recce party had in fact been

One of the curiosities discovered by the US 29th Infantry Division at the Luftwaffe's Karlwitz munitions depot near Dannenberg in April 1945 were these incomplete Fi-103Re.4 piloted V1 'flying bombs'. The fairing that sat behind the cockpit canopy can be seen at bottom right. (NARA)

captured and interrogated, and a reception had been prepared; the Arado was forced to divert to an alternative landing site, where it crash-landed. The agents made their way towards Moscow using a motorcycle with sidecar that had been carried in the aircraft, leaving the aircrew to make a forlorn attempt to reach German-held territory. The would-be assassins were arrested at a checkpoint; whether their mission ever had the remotest chance of success is impossible to say, but the whole operation is typical of the kind of wild plans with which KG 200 often became involved.

Towards the end of the war, Baumbach was promoted Oberst and left KG 200 to become the General der Kampfflieger or Inspector-General of Bomber Aircrew, the highest-ranking appointment in the bomber arm.

One of the few piloted V1s found with its intended warhead, near Rheinmetall's Hillersleben artillery proving ground, on its TW-76 trolley. Its wings are stacked near the side of the rail car and show the ailerons that were added to this version of the missile for manual control. (USAOM-APG).

One example of the *Mistel* combination, as operated by 7./ KG 200. The 'piggy-back' fighter sitting in the attachment cradle is a Focke-Wulf Fw190, but the Messerschmitt Bf109 was also used. (Thomas Huss)

SUMMARY

During the first part of the war the Brandenburger*s* were Germany's only special forces troops, and although they did not achieve every objective they were set they had significant successes in *coup de main* missions during offensive operations. As Germany's advances on all fronts first slowed and then stalled, their value lay mostly in deep reconnaissance missions. As the tide of war began to turn the Brandenburgers increasingly found themselves employed for operations that wasted their special skills and, with rising casualties, diluted them. With the final eclipse of their controlling organization, the Abwehr, at the hands of the SS, the Brandenburgers were unrealistically expanded and largely relegated to the status of an ordinary combat unit.

Simultaneously, the SD-controlled SS units led by Otto Skorzeny became the prime force in German special operations. Skorzeny's SS-Jagdverbände would also achieve some eye-catching successes, but these achievements brought few strategic rewards and represented little more than a few positive interludes during a relentless series of military defeats and disasters. The special forces units of the Kriegsmarine, formed only in 1944, at least equalled their land comrades in courage and commitment, but had no significant influence on the course of the war. The Luftwaffe's KG 200 carried out useful clandestine missions, and employed some innovative weapons systems, of which the world's first 'smart bombs' – while technically immature – were by far the most significant and successful.

In sum, it may be argued that during the early part of the war German special forces justified their existence with a number of successful operations, most of which were necessarily kept secret. During the second half of the war, although they had no significant effect on the outcome of conventional operations, those audacious exploits that were publicized by the propaganda machine did provide Germany with much-needed boosts to morale. In comparison with the massive waste of resources incurred by the Nazi regime over a diverse and overly complex range of proposed weapons systems, it may reasonably be argued that Germany's special forces did justify their existence in terms of both military success and propaganda value.

SELECT BIBLIOGRAPHY

Blocksdorf, Helmut, *Das Kommando Kleinkampfverbände der Kriegsmarine*, Motorbuch Verlag, 2003

Foley, John, *Commando Extraordinary: Otto Skorzeny*, Cassell, 1998

Jung, Michael, *Sabotage unter Wasser – Die deutschen Kampfschwimmer im Zweiten Weltkrieg*, Verlag E. S. Mittler & Sohn, Hamburg, 2004

Kunzmann, Adolf & Milius, Siegfried, *Fallschirmjäger der Waffen-SS im Bild*, Munin Verlag, 1986

Lefevre, Eric, *Brandenburg Division: Commandos of the Reich*, Histoire & Collections, 2000

Luther, Craig and Taylor, *Hugh Page, For Germany – The Skorzeny Memoirs*, Bender Publishing, 2005

Michaelis, Rolf, *SS-Fallschirmjäger Battalion 500/600*, Schiffer Publishing, 2008

Molinari, Andrea, *Battle Orders 23: Desert Raiders: Allied & Axis Special Forces 1940–43*, Osprey Publishing, 2007

Pallud, John-Paul *Elite 11: Ardennes 1944 – Peiper & Skorzeny*, Osprey Publishing, 1987

Rössler, Eberhard, *The U-Boat*, Cassell & Co., 1981

Stahl, Peter, *KG200: The True Story*, Jane's Publishing, 1981

Tarrant, V. E., *The Last Year of the Kriegsmarine, May 1944–May 1945*, Arms & Armour Press, 1994

Westwell, Ian, *Brandenburgers – The Third Reich's Special Forces*, Ian Allan, 2003

INDEX